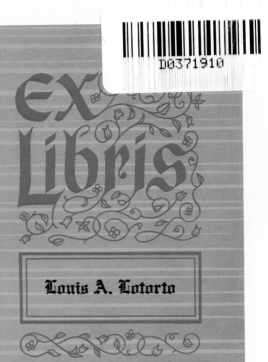

SHERLOCK HOLMES

SHERLOCK HOLMES

A Play

by

WILLIAM GILLETTE

and

SIR ARTHUR CONAN DOYLE

Doubleday & Company, Inc.
Garden City, New York

SHERLOCK HOLMES

Cast

MADGE LARRABEE	BILLY
JOHN FORMAN	DR. WATSON
JAMES LARRABEE	JIM CRAIGIN
TÉRÈSE	THOMAS LEARY
SIDNEY PRINCE	"LIGHTFOOT" Mc TAGUE
ALICE FAULKNER	MRS. SMEEDLEY
SHERLOCK HOLMES	PARSONS
PROFESSOR MORIARTY	COUNT VON STALBURG
JOHN	SIR EDWARD LEIGHTON
ALFRED BASSICK	THE KING OF BOHEMIA

ACT I

Scene 1

Drawing room at the Larrabees'. Evening.

Scene 2

Professor Moriarty's Underground Office. Morning.

Scene 3

Sherlock Holmes's Apartments in Baker Street. Evening.

ACT II

Scene 1

The Stepney Gas Chamber. Midnight.

Scene 2

Dr. Watson's Consulting Room, Kensington. The following evening.

The place is London.

ACT I

Scene 1

The scene represents the drawing room at Edelweiss Lodge, an old house, gloomy and decayed, situated in a lonely district in a little frequented part of London.

The furniture is old and decayed, with the exception of the piano—a baby grand. The desk is very solid. The ceiling is heavily beamed. Many places out of repair in the walls and ceilings. Carvings broken here and there.

The music stops an instant before RISE OF CURTAIN. *A short pause after curtain is up.* CURTAIN RISES *in darkness*—LIGHTS COME UP. MADGE LARRABEE *is discovered up R.C., anxiously waiting. A strikingly handsome woman, but with a somewhat hard face. Black hair. Richly dressed.*

Enter FORMAN *at door C. with evening paper. He is a quiet, perfectly trained servant. He comes down C. and is met by* MADGE, *who takes the paper from him quickly.*

FORMAN

(Speaks always very quietly)

Pardon, ma'am, but one of the maids wishes to speak to you.

*(*MADGE *is scanning the paper eagerly and sinks onto seat at the foot of the piano)*

MADGE

(*Not looking from paper*)

I can't spare the time now.

FORMAN

Very well, ma'am.

(*Turns to go*)

MADGE

(*Without looking up from paper*)

Which maid was it?

FORMAN

(*Turning toward* MADGE *again*)

Térèse, ma'am.

MADGE

(*Looking up. Very slight surprise in her tone*)

Térèse!

FORMAN

Yes, ma'am.

MADGE

Have you any idea what she wants?

FORMAN

Not the least, ma'am.

MADGE

She must tell you. I'm very busy, and I can't see her unless I know.

FORMAN

I'll say so, ma'am.

(Turns and exits C., carefully and quietly closing the door after him—immediately coming in again and watching MADGE *from up C.*

MADGE *busy with paper. Finds what she has been looking for, and starts eagerly to read it. As if not seeing the print well she leans near light, and resumes reading with the greatest avidity.* FORMAN *quietly shuts door up C. He stands at the door looking at* MADGE *as she reads the paper. This is prolonged somewhat, so that it may be seen that he is not waiting for her to finish from mere politeness. His eyes are upon her sharply and intensely, yet he does not assume any expression otherwise. She finishes and angrily rises, casting the paper violently down on the piano. She turns and goes over to R., near the large, heavy desk. Pauses there. Then turns away to L. angrily. Sees* FORMAN, *calms herself at once. Just as* MADGE *turns,* FORMAN *seems to be coming into the room and moves down a little near C.)*

FORMAN

(Half down C.)

I could get nothing from her, ma'am. She insists that she must speak to you herself.

MADGE

Tell her to wait till tomorrow.

(Turns and moves toward R.)

FORMAN

I asked her to do that, ma'am, and she said that she would not be here tomorrow.

*(*MADGE *turns toward* FORMAN *with some surprise.*

FORMAN bows and turns to go. MADGE goes toward the piano near where the paper lies. She sees it. Stops with hand on piano)

Judson! How did you happen to imagine that I would be interested in this marriage announcement?

(FORMAN stops and comes down. Everything quiet, subdued, catlike in his methods. MADGE takes up paper and sits in seat below the piano)

FORMAN

(C.)

I could 'ardly 'elp it, ma'am.

(MADGE turns and looks hard at him an instant. FORMAN stands deferentially)

MADGE

I suppose you have overheard certain references to the matter—between myself and my brother?

FORMAN

I 'ave, ma'am, but I would never have referred to it in the least if I did not think it might be of some importance to you, ma'am.

MADGE

Oh no—of no special importance! We know the parties concerned, and are naturally interested in the event. Of course, you do not imagine there is anything more.

(She does not look at him as she says this)

FORMAN

(Not looking at MADGE—eyes front)

Certainly not, ma'am. Anyway, if I did imagine there was something more, I'm sure

(Looks L.)

You would find it to your interest, ma'am, to remember my faithful services in helpin' to keep it quiet.

MADGE

(*After slight pause, during which she looks steadily in front*)

Judson, what sort of a fool are you? You are a self-confessed forger.

FORMAN

(*Quick movement of apprehension*)

No!

(*Apprehensive look around*)

Don't speak out like that!

(*Recovers a little*)

It was—it was in confidence—I told you in confidence, ma'am.

MADGE

Well, I'm telling you in confidence that at the first sign of any underhand conduct on *your* part this little episode of yours will—

FORMAN

(*Hurriedly—to prevent her from speaking it*)

Yes, yes! I will—bear it in mind, ma'am. I will bear it in mind!

MADGE

(*After a sharp look at him as if satisfying herself that he is now reduced to proper condition*)

Very well . . .

(*Moves down R.*)

Now, as to the maid—Térèse—

(FORMAN, *near C.—inclines head for instruction*)

Can you explain why she says she will not be here tomorrow?

FORMAN

(*His eyes turn away from* MADGE. *Speaking in low tones, and behavior subdued as if completely humiliated*)

It has occurred to me, ma'am, that she may have taken exceptions to some occurrences which she thinks she 'as seen going on in this 'ouse.

MADGE

I'll raise her wages. If it isn't money that she wants—I'll see her myself.

FORMAN

Very well, ma'am.

(*He turns and exits quietly up C.*

MADGE *stands motionless a moment. There is a sound of a heavy door outside L. opening and closing.* MADGE *gives a quick motion of listening. Hurries to L., looking off. Enter* JIM LARRABEE, *through archway, passing her to C. in some excitement. He is a tall, heavily built man, with a hard face. Full of determination and a strong character. He is well dressed, and attractive in some respects. A fine looking man. Dark hair and eyes, but the hard, sinister look of a criminal*)

LARRABEE

Have you seen this?

MADGE

Yes. Didn't you find Sid?

LARRABEE

No.

(*Goes to the heavy desk safe at R. and throws open the wooden doors of lower part, showing the iron and*

*combination lock of a safe or strongbox. Gives knob a
turn or two nervously, and works at it.*

MADGE *follows to R.C. up near piano watching him*)

LARRABEE (*Continued*)

He wasn't there!

(*Rises from desk and goes R.C.*)

We'll have to get a locksmith in.

MADGE

(*Quickly*)

No, no! We can't do that! It isn't safe!

(*R.C. below piano*)

LARRABEE

(*Turning at R.*)

We've got to do something, haven't we?

(*Stoops down quickly before door of safe again, and
nervously tries it. Busy at safe*)

There's no time to waste, either! They've put Holmes on the
case!

MADGE

Sherlock Holmes?

LARRABEE

Yes.

MADGE

What could he do?

LARRABEE

(*Rises and faces her*)

I don't know—but he'll make some move—he never waits long!

(Moves about restlessly on the R. but stops when MADGE *speaks)*

MADGE

Can't you think of someone else—as we can't find Sid?

(Goes up slightly L.C.)

LARRABEE

He may turn up yet. I left word with Billy Rounds, and he's on the hunt for him.

(Between his teeth)

Oh! it's damnable. After holding on for two good years just for this and now the time comes and she's blocked us!

LARRABEE *(Continued)*

(Goes to and looks off and up stairway. Looks at MADGE. *Goes to her)*

Look here! I'll just get at her for a moment.

(Starting toward L.)

I have an idea I can change her mind.

MADGE

(Quickly)

No, wait, Jim.

*(*LARRABEE *stops and turns to her. She goes near him)*

What's the use of hurting the girl? We've tried all that!

LARRABEE

Well, I'll try something else!

(Turns and goes to archway)

MADGE

(Quick, half whisper)

Jim!

*(*LARRABEE *turns,* MADGE *approaches him)*

Remember—nothing that'll show! No marks!

LARRABEE

(*Going doggedly*)

I'll look out for that.

(*Exit* LARRABEE, *running upstairs in haste. As* MADGE *looks after him with a trifle of anxiety standing in arch-way, enter* TÉRÈSE *up C. She is a quiet-looking French maid with a pleasant face. She stands near the door up C.* MADGE *turns into the room and sees her. Stands an instant. She moves toward C. and seats herself in the armchair L.C.*)

MADGE

Come here. Come here!

(TÉRÈSE *comes down a little way—with slight hesitation*)

Now, what is it?

TÉRÈSE

Meester Judson said I vas to come.

MADGE

I told Judson to arrange with you himself.

TÉRÈSE

He could not, madame. I do not veesh longer to remain.

MADGE

What is it? You must give me some reason!

TÉRÈSE

It is zat I wish to go.

MADGE

You've been here months, and have made no complaint.

TÉRÈSE

Ah, madame—it is not so before! It is now beginning zat I do not like.

MADGE

(*Rising*)

What? What is it you do not like?

TÉRÈSE

(*With some little spirit but low voice*)

I do not like eet, madame—eet—here—zis place—what you do —ze young lady you have up zere! I cannot remain to see!

(*Indicating above*)

Eet eez not well! I cannot remain to see!

MADGE

You know nothing about it! The young lady is ill. She is not right here—

(*Touching forehead*)

She is a great trouble to us, but we take every care of her, and treat her with the utmost kindness and—

(*Scream off*)

Don't be alarmed, my dear, poor Miss Faulkner's head is very bad today. But she'll be better soon.

(*A piercing scream, as if muffled by something, heard in distant part of house above*)

Wait here. Don't leave the room.

(*Enter* FORMAN *quietly at door up C. He looks toward L. a moment where* MADGE *has just taken the* OLD LADY *off.* TÉRÈSE *is looking also the same way from down stage.* FORMAN *goes down to* TÉRÈSE. *They look at one another an instant in silence. Then he speaks to her in a low voice*)

FORMAN

She's made it quite satisfactory, I suppose.

(TÉRÈSE *looks at* FORMAN)

You will not leave her—now?

(*Turning R. a little*)

I can find another place; eet eez not so *difficile*.

FORMAN

(*Remains R.C.*)

Not so *difficile* if you know where to go!

TÉRÈSE

(*R.*)

Ah—zhat eez it!

FORMAN

(*Moves to her*)

Here—on this card—

(*Quickly takes card from pocket and pushes it into her hands*)

Go to that address! Don't let anyone see it!

(*Looks L.*)

TÉRÈSE

(*Quickly looking at card while* FORMAN *looks away to L. —Begins slowly to read*)

Meester—Sheer-lock—

FORMAN

(*With a quick warning exclamation, and sudden turn, seizes her, covering her mouth with one hand; they stand a moment, he looks slowly around to L.*)

Someone might hear you! Go to that address in the morning.

(The front-door bell rings. Bell off L. FORMAN motions her off with quick short motion. She exits door up C. around piano. FORMAN exits up L. to open the house door—quickly. Sound of house door opening outside L.—a solid heavy sound—not sharp. Enter SID PRINCE, L. walking in quickly. He is a short, stoutish, dapper little fellow. He carries a small black satchel, wears overcoat and hat, gloves, etc., and is well dressed and jaunty. He wears diamond scarf pin, rings, etc., is quick in movements and always on the alert. FORMAN follows him on, standing near archway at L.)

PRINCE

(Going across toward piano)

Don't waste time, you fool; tell 'em it's Mr. Sidney Prince, Esquire.

(He puts satchel, which is apparently heavy, on seat at foot of piano)

FORMAN

Oh, yes, sir—I beg your *pardon!* I'll announce you immediate, sir.

(Exits upstairs.

PRINCE *takes off hat, gloves, etc., laying them so as to cover the satchel. Looks about room. Walks over to the heavy desk R. and glances at it. Swings lower door of the desk open in easy businesslike way)*

PRINCE

Ah!

(As if he had found what he was looking for. Not an exclamation of surprise. Drops on one knee and gives the lock a turn. Rises and goes over to his satchel—

*which he uncovers and opens. Feels about for some-
thing.*

MADGE *and* LARRABEE *come downstairs and enter L.*
PRINCE *sees them, but does not stop what he is doing*)

MADGE

(*Going across to* PRINCE)

Oh, is that you, Sid? I'm so glad you've come.

LARRABEE

Hello, Sid . . .

(*Quick "Sh!" from* MADGE *just behind him*)

LARRABEE

(*At the same time*)

Shut up!

(*They look around.* MADGE *goes to C.* PRINCE *looks up
surprised*)

For heaven's sake, Sid, remember—

(*Down to* PRINCE)

—*my* name is Chetwood here.

PRINCE

Beg your pardon. My mistake. Old times when we was learnin'
the trade together—eh!

LARRABEE

Yes, yes!

PRINCE

I 'ardly expected you'd be doin' the 'igh tone thing over 'ere,
when I first come up with you workin' the card tables on the
Carmania out o' New York.

LARRABEE

We don't have to go into that now.

PRINCE

There's no need to get so 'uffy about it! All clear, you say? No danger lurking?

LARRABEE

(*Shaking head*)

Not the least!

(MADGE *moves away a little to L.C. glancing cautiously about.* PRINCE *tries tools.* LARRABEE *remains near piano R.C. Both watch him as he tries tools in the lock*)

PRINCE

(*At lock*)

You're not robbing *yourselves,* I trust?

LARRABEE

(*Near* PRINCE)

It does look a little like it!

PRINCE

I knew you was on some rum lay—squatting down in this place for over a year; but I never could seem to—

(*Business*)

—get a line on you.

(*He works a moment, then crosses to get a tool out of satchel, and goes near light on piano and begins to adjust it. This must bring him where he commands stage, up R.C. a little. Stopping and looking sharply at* MADGE *and* LARRABEE)

PRINCE (*Continued*)

What do we get here? It's not fifty thousand pounds in notes, by any chance?

LARRABEE

(*R.*)

Sorry to disappoint you, but it isn't.

PRINCE

That's too bad.

(*R.C. near lamp at piano.*

PRINCE *works at tool an instant before speaking*)

Papers!

LARRABEE

Yes.

PRINCE

Now 'ere. We go, then.

(*Glances around quickly*)

Before we starts 'er goin' however what's the general surround-in's?

LARRABEE

What's the good of wasting time on this?

(*Going near* PRINCE)

PRINCE

(*Up to him*)

If I'm in this, I'm in it, ain't I? An' I want to know *wot* I'm in.

MADGE

Why don't you tell him, Jimmie?

PRINCE

If anything 'appened, 'ow'd I let the office know 'oo to look out for?

LARRABEE

Now, Sid.

> (MADGE *goes up to arch.*
>
> *Nearer* PRINCE *and speaking lower*)

You know we've been working the Continent. Pleasure palaces and all that.

PRINCE

So I've 'eard.

> (MADGE *motions them to wait. Looking off quietly.*
> *Nods them to proceed. Remaining L.C.*)

LARRABEE

It was over there—a place called Bad Homburg in Bohemia. We ran across a young girl who'd been havin' trouble. Sister just died, no parents. Madge took hold and found that this sister of hers had been having some kind of a love affair with a—well— with a foreign gentleman of exceedingly high rank—

PRINCE

A foreign gentleman!

LARRABEE

That's what I said.

PRINCE

'Ow much was there to it?

LARRABEE

Promise of marriage.

PRINCE

Broke it, of course.

LARRABEE

Of course—and her heart with it. I don't know what more she expected—anyway, she *did* expect more and she and her child died together.

PRINCE

Oh—dead!

(MADGE *turns to* LARRABEE *and* PRINCE *and listens*)

LARRABEE

Yes, but the case isn't; there's evidence—letter, photographs, jewelry with inscriptions that he gave her. Now the sister's been keeping them and . . . we've been keeping the sister . . .

PRINCE

An' what's 'er little game?

LARRABEE

To get even.

PRINCE

An' your little game?

LARRABEE

(*Shrug of shoulders*)

Whatever there is in it.

PRINCE

These letters an' things ought to be worth a little something!

LARRABEE

I tell you it wouldn't be safe for him to marry until he's got them out of the way! He knows that perfectly well. But what's more, the *family* knows it!

PRINCE

Oh—family! . . . Rich, I take it.

LARRABEE

Rich isn't quite the word. They're something else.

(LARRABEE *moves nearer* PRINCE *and whispers a name in his ear*)

PRINCE

My Gawd! Royalty itself, eh? Which one of 'em?

LARRABEE

(*Shakes head*)

We can't tell you that.

PRINCE

Well, we *are* a-movin' among the swells now, ain't we? But this 'ere girl—the one whose sister died—'ow did you manage to get 'er into it?

MADGE

(*Moving near at C.*)

I picked her up of course and consoled her. I invited her to stay with me at my house in London. Jimmy came over and took this place—and when I brought her across a week later everything was all ready—and a private desk safe for the letters and jewelry.

LARRABEE

(*Turning*)

Yes—combination, lock and all . . . well, everything worked smooth until a couple of weeks ago, when we began to hear from a firm of London solicitors, some veiled proposals were made—now this showed the time was coming. They wanted the stuff out of the way. Then suddenly all negotiations on their side stopped. Well, the next thing for me to do was to threaten. But I needed the letters for that, but when I went to get them—I found that in some way the girl had managed to change the lock on us. The numbers were all wrong—and we couldn't starve or frighten her into opening the thing.

PRINCE

You've got the stuff in there!

LARRABEE

That's what I'm telling you, Sid, it's in there and she juggled the lock.

PRINCE

Oh, well, it won't take long to rectify that triflin' error.
(*Stops at R. looking front*)
But wot puzzles *me* is w'y the solicitors broke off with their offers that way.

LARRABEE

(*Goes nearer to* PRINCE)
That's simple enough.
(PRINCE *turns to him for explanation*)
They gave it up themselves, and got in Sherlock Holmes.

PRINCE

(*Suddenly starting*)
Wot's that!
(*Pause*)
Is 'Olmes in this?

LARRABEE

That's what they told me!

MADGE

But what can he *do,* Sid?

PRINCE

Never mind about that—I'll get the safe open.
(*Goes to piano in front of* LARRABEE)
You send a telegram, that's all I ask!

(Tears page out of his notebook and writes hurriedly. The other two watch him. LARRABEE remaining at R. a little suspiciously. Silence for a few moments while he writes)

Where's your nearest telegraph office?

MADGE

Round the corner.

(Going to above piano)

PRINCE

(Down to LARRABEE and giving him the telegram he has written)

Right. Run for it! Mark what I say—*run for it.*

(LARRABEE is looking at him hard)

That's to Alf Bassick. He's Professor Moriarty's confidential man. Moriarty is king—in London, he runs everything that's shady—an' 'Olmes 'as been settin' lines all round 'im for months—and he didn't know it—an' now he's beginnin' to find out that 'Olmes is trackin' 'im down—and there's the devil to pay.

LARRABEE

What are you telling him?

PRINCE

Nothing whatever, except I've got a job on I want to see 'im about in the mornin' . . . Read it yourself.

(LARRABEE looks at what PRINCE has written)

But don't take all night over it! We cawn't tell wot might 'appen.

(Crosses to safe R.)

MADGE

Go on, Jim!

(LARRABEE *crosses to L.,* MADGE *following him*)

LARRABEE

(*To* MADGE *near archway*)

Keep your eyes open.

MADGE

(*To* LARRABEE)

Don't you worry!

(*Exit* LARRABEE.

MADGE *is looking after him. Quick sound of door closing outside L. As* LARRABEE *and* MADGE *moved L.,* PRINCE *dropped down to work—real work now—at desk R. Short pause.* MADGE *stands watching* PRINCE *a moment up L. She moves over to near piano R.C., and picks up a book carelessly, which she glances at with perfect nonchalance. After a time she speaks without taking eyes from book*)

I've heard of this Professor Moriarty.

(*Above piano, leaning on it*)

What does he do?

PRINCE

I'll tell you one thing he does! He's the Emperor!

(*Turns to her and rests a moment from work*)

He sits at 'ome—quiet and easy—runs nearly every big operation that's on. All the clever boys are under him one way or another —an' he 'olds them in 'is 'and without moving a muscle! An' if there should be a slip and the police get wind of it, there ain't never any 'old on 'im. They can't touch him. And wot's more, they wouldn't want to touch him if they could.

MADGE

Why not?

PRINCE

Because they've tried it—that's w'y—an' the men as did try it was found shortly after a-floatin' in the river—that is, if they was ever found at all! Once a man's marked by Moriarty there ain't a street that's safe for 'im!

(*Resumes drilling.*

PRINCE *works rapidly, drill going in suddenly as if he had one hole sunk. He tries a few tools in it and quickly starts another hole with drills.* MADGE *starts forward at business of drill*)

MADGE

(*Recovering to careless*)

Have you got it, Sid?

PRINCE

Not yet—but I know where I am now. I'll be there soon.

(*Sound of door closing outside L. Enter* LARRABEE *L., hurriedly. He is breathless from running*)

LARRABEE

Well, now, Sid. How goes it?

(*At C.*)

PRINCE

(*Working*)

So-so.

LARRABEE

Now about this Professor Moriarty?

(*Gets chair from near piano, and sits behind* PRINCE)

PRINCE

(*Working*)

Ask 'er.

MADGE

(*Down to him on his R.*)

It's all right, Jim. It was the proper thing to do.

(*Music. Melodramatic, very soft. Hardly audible.*

MADGE and LARRABEE move near PRINCE, looking over him eagerly. He quickly introduces small punch and hammers rapidly; sound of bolts, etc., falling inside lock as if loosened. Eagerness of all three increases with final sound of loose ironwork inside lock, and PRINCE at once pulls open the iron doors. All three give a quick look within. MADGE and LARRABEE start back with subdued exclamations. PRINCE looks in more carefully, then turns to them. Pause. LARRABEE in moving back pushes a chair along with him. Pause. Music stops)

MADGE (*Continued*)

(*Turning to LARRABEE on her L.*)

Ah! Gone!

LARRABEE

(*To MADGE*)

She's taken 'em out!

PRINCE

(*Rising to his feet*)

What do you mean?

LARRABEE

The girl!

(*MADGE stops and goes quickly to safe R. in front of PRINCE, and dropping down feels carefully about inside. Others watch her closely. PRINCE gives back a little for her.*

NOTE: *Their dialogue since opening of safe has dropped to low, excited tones, almost whispers, as they would if it were a robbery. Force of habit in their intense excitement*)

MADGE

(*Rises and turns to* LARRABEE)

She's got them!

PRINCE

She wants to get even, you say.

MADGE

Yes! yes!

PRINCE

Well, then, if she's got the thing out of the box there—ain't it quite likely she's sent 'em along to the girl as 'is royal highness wants to marry.

(*Brief pause*)

MADGE

No! She hasn't had the chance.

LARRABEE

She couldn't get them out of this room. We've watched her too close for that.

MADGE

Wait!

(*Strides toward archway*)

I'll get her down! She'll tell us where they are or strangle for it!

(*Turns hurriedly*)

Now you wait here! When I get her down, don't give her time to think!

(Exit LARRABEE *L.* PRINCE *comes to the end of the piano, looking after* LARRABEE.
Music. Very soft.
Brief pause. MADGE *glances nervously L.)*

PRINCE

(R.C.)

Wot's he goin' to do?

MADGE

(R.)

We've got to get it out of her or the whole two years' work is wasted. So there's only one thing he can do.

(Muffled cry of pain from ALICE *in distance, outside up.* MADGE *crosses to L.C. going in front of* PRINCE *nervously. Pause)*

PRINCE

(Glances off L. anxiously)

Look 'ere, I don't so much fancy that sort of thing.

(Goes to safe and collects tools)

Torture, and that.

MADGE

(Up L.C.)

Don't you worry, we'll attend to it!

PRINCE

Well, I suppose there are more ways of killing a cat than drowning it with cream. If your 'eart's set on it, that is.

MADGE

Yes, for two years . . .

(LARRABEE *brings* ALICE *on.* ALICE *at a little L. of C.
motionless.* MADGE *up L.C.* LARRABEE *at L., well down.*
PRINCE *down R.C.*)

LARRABEE

Now we'll see whether you will or not.

(NOTE: *This scene should be played well upstage.*
Music stops.
Coming down)

Now tell her what we want.

ALICE

(*Low voice—slight shake of head*)

You needn't tell me, I know well enough.

MADGE

(*Drawing nearer to* ALICE *with quiet, catlike glide
down on* ALICE's *L. Smiling*)

Oh no, dear, you don't know. It isn't anything to do with locks,
or keys, or numbers this time.

(*Points slowly to the open safe at R.*)

We want to know what you've done with them!

(*Pause.* ALICE *looks at* MADGE *calmly. No defiance or
suffering in her expression.*
Comes closer and speaks with set teeth)

Do you hear! We want to know what you've done with them.

ALICE

(*Low voice—but clear and distinct*)

You will not know from me.

LARRABEE

(*Moves toward her*)

You're going to tell us what you've done with that package before you leave this room tonight!

(MADGE *backs away L. a step or two*)

ALICE

Not if you kill me.

LARRABEE

(*Seizing* ALICE *violently by the arms or wrists at back of her*)

It isn't killing that's going to do it—it's something else.

(*Music melodramatic and pathetic.*

LARRABEE *gets* ALICE'S *arms behind her, and holds her as if wrenching or twisting them from behind. She gives a slight cry of pain.* MADGE *comes to her on her L.* PRINCE *looks away to R. during following business—appearing not to like the scene but not moving*)

MADGE

(*Sharp, hard voice*)

Tell us where it is! Tell us and he'll stop.

(*A little behind-business of gripping as if wrenching her arms*)

Out with it!

(NOTE: ALICE *has little expression of pain on her face. The idea is to be game*)

MADGE

Where is it?

LARRABEE

Where is it? I'll give you a turn next time that'll take it out of you. Where is it?

MADGE

(*Low voice*)

Be careful, Jimmie!

LARRABEE

(*Angry*)

Is this any time to be careful?

(*Business*)

Will you tell?

(*Business*)

Will you—

(*Loud ringing of door bell in distant part of house.* NOTE: *This must on no account be close at hand. After bell music stops, quick turn on ring*)

PRINCE

(*Short, sharp whisper as he starts up*)

Look out!

(*All stand listening an instant.* ALICE, *however, has heard nothing, as the pain has made her faint, though not unconscious.* MADGE *L.C. by chair.* LARRABEE *pushes* ALICE *into chair upstage facing fireplace. He then hides her.* MADGE *goes quickly down L. side and cautiously draws picture from a small concealed window on extreme L. down stage.* LARRABEE *stands near* ALICE *close up on her L. Steps heard outside L.* LARRABEE *turns quickly to L., hearing steps. Make these steps distinct—slow—not loud*)

LARRABEE

(*Speaking off L.*)

Here!

(*Enter* FORMAN *L. He stands waiting*)

Don't go to that door; see who it is.

(FORMAN *simply waits—no surprise on his face.* MADGE *turning at L. and speaking in low but clear voice.* LARRABEE *stands so that* FORMAN *will not see* ALICE)

MADGE

(*Standing on ottoman L.*)

Tall, slim man—long coat—soft hat—smooth face—carries . . . an ebony cane—

(*Short, quick exclamation from* PRINCE)

PRINCE

(*Breaks in with quick exclamation under breath.* MADGE *stopped by* PRINCE'*s exclamation*)

Sherlock 'Olmes! 'E's 'ere!

(*Pause.* PRINCE *quickly conceals his satchel at R. above safe—also closing door of safe. Music, melodramatic, very soft*)

LARRABEE

(*R.C., moving toward piano, turns out lamp*)

We won't answer the bell.

PRINCE

No! That man, he's got hypernatural powers! He knows what the rats are thinking in the cellars!

LARRABEE

Nonsense.

PRINCE

Hide the girl. Get her away! Quick!

LARRABEE

Well, I suppose if we have to answer the bell . . .

PRINCE

It's your only hope!

LARRABEE

Take her up the back stairway!

(MADGE *takes* ALICE *quickly and forces her to door up C. as they speak*)

MADGE

(*Stopping up C. to speak to* LARRABEE *and speaking out very distinctly*)

She's in poor health and can't see anyone—*you understand.*

LARRABEE

Yes! yes! Lock her in the room—and stay by the door.

(MADGE *and* ALICE *quickly exit at door up C. which* LARRABEE *closes at once and stands an instant uncertain. There he goes to and opens lid of box on R. of wall seat, and gets a loaded club—an ugly-looking weapon—and shoves it into* PRINCE's *hand at up R.C.*)

Sid, you get out there!

(*Indicating up R.*)

Keep quiet there till he gets in the house—then come round to the front. Be ready for 'im when he comes out! If he gets the stuff in spite of us, I'll give you two sharp whistles! If you don't hear it, let him pass.

PRINCE

But if I *do* 'ear the two whistles—?

LARRABEE

Then let 'im have it.

PRINCE

Oh, my Gawd . . .

(PRINCE *gets off at window up R., which he closes at once.* LARRABEE *moves rapidly down R. kicking door of desk shut as he passes. Stands at piano R.C. leaning on it carelessly. Turns to* FORMAN)

FORMAN

Sir?

LARRABEE

Go on, answer the bell.

(FORMAN *bows slightly and exits* L. LARRABEE *strolls about trying to get into an assumption of coolness. Picks up book off piano. Sound of heavy door closing outside* L. *Brief pause. Enter* SHERLOCK HOLMES *at* L., *hat and stick in hand—wearing a long coat, or ulster, and gloves. He lingers in the archway, apparently seeing nothing in particular, and slowly drawing off gloves. Then moves to wall seat close at hand and sits. Music stops.*

After quite a time LARRABEE *turns at* R., *throws book on piano, and saunters toward* HOLMES *in rather an ostentatious manner*)

LARRABEE (*Continued*)

Ah, Mr. Holmes, I believe.

HOLMES

(*Rises and turns to* LARRABEE *as if mildly surprised*)

LARRABEE

Who did you wish to see, Mr. Holmes?

HOLMES

(*Looking steadily at* LARRABEE *an instant. Speaks very quietly*)

Thank you so much—I sent my card—by the butler.

LARRABEE

(*Stands motionless an instant—after an instant's pause*)

Oh—very well.

(Turns and strolls R.C.

Long pause. Enter FORMAN *down stairs.* LARRABEE
moves up near piano and turns to hear what FORMAN
says)

FORMAN

(To HOLMES*)*

Miss Faulkner begs Mr. Holmes to excuse her. She is not well
enough to see anyone this evening.

*(*HOLMES *takes out notebook and pencil and writes a
word or two on a card or leaf of the book. Tears it out
of letter. Pulls out watch and glances at it. Hands the
card to* FORMAN, *taking off coat first)*

HOLMES

Hand that to Miss Faulkner—and say . . .

LARRABEE

(At R.C. near piano)

I beg your pardon, Mr. Holmes, but it's quite useless—really.

HOLMES

Oh—I'm so sorry to hear it.

*(*HOLMES *turns quietly to* LARRABEE *and looks at him.*
LARRABEE *is a trifle affected by* HOLMES*'s quiet scru-
tiny)*

LARRABEE

Yes—Miss Faulkner is—I regret to say—quite an invalid. She is
unable to see anyone—her health is so poor.

HOLMES

Did it ever occur to you that she might be confined to the house
too much?

(An instant's pause)

LARRABEE

(*Suddenly in low, threatening tone but not too violent*)

How does that concern you?

HOLMES

(*Easily*)

It doesn't—I simply made the suggestion.

(*The two look at one another an instant.* HOLMES *turns quietly to* FORMAN.)

That's all.

(*Motions him slightly*)

Go on. Take it up.

(*Exit* FORMAN *at L. and up stairway. After a moment* LARRABEE *turns, goes down R.C., breaking into hearty laughter*)

LARRABEE

Ha! ha!

(*Strolling off to R. laughing*)

Well, of *course* he can take up your card—or your note—or whatever it is, if you wish it so much; I was only trying to save you the trouble.

HOLMES

(*Who has been watching him through foregoing speech*)

Thanks—hardly any trouble at all to send a card.

(*Seats himself in an easy, languid way—picks up Punch*)

LARRABEE

(*Turning at R.C. endeavors to be easy, careless, and patronizing*)

Do you know, Mr. Holmes, you interest me very much.

HOLMES

(*Easily*)

Ah!

LARRABEE

Upon my word, yes! We've all heard of your wonderful methods.

(*Coming toward* HOLMES)

Your marvelous insight—your ingenuity in picking up and following clues—and the astonishing manner in which you gain information from the most trifling details . . . why, I dare say—in this brief moment or two you've discovered any number of things about me.

HOLMES

Nothing of consequence, Mr. Chetwood—I have scarcely more than asked myself why you rushed off and sent that telegram in such a frightened hurry—what possible excuse you could have had for gulping down a tumbler of raw brandy at the Lion's Head on the way back—why your friend left by the terrace window so suddenly—and what there can possibly be about the safe in the lower part of that desk to cause you such painful anxiety.

(*Pause.* LARRABEE *standing motionless looking at* HOLMES. HOLMES *picks up paper and reads*)

LARRABEE

Ha! ha! very good! Very good indeed! If those things were only true now, I should be wonderfully impressed.

(*He breaks off as* FORMAN *enters—coming downstairs. He quietly crosses to* LARRABEE, *who is watching him and extends salver with a note upon it.* HOLMES *is looking over paper languidly.* LARRABEE *takes note.* FORMAN *retires up L.C.*)

You'll forgive me, I trust.

(HOLMES *remains silent, glancing over paper and looking quietly at* FORMAN. LARRABEE *reads the note hastily.*

First a second's thought after reading, as he sees that HOLMES *is not observing him—then speaking*)

Ah—this is from—Miss Faulkner! Well, really! She begs to be allowed to see—Mr. Holmes. She absolutely *implores* it!

(HOLMES *looks slowly up as though scarcely interested*)

LARRABEE (*Continued*)

Well, I suppose I shall just have to give way.

(*Turns to* FORMAN *R.C.*)

Oh, Judson!

FORMAN

Sir.

LARRABEE

(*Emphasizing words in italics*)

Ask Miss Faulkner to come down to the drawing room. Say that Mr. Holmes is waiting to see her.

FORMAN

Very good, sir.

(*Bows and exits upstairs*)

LARRABEE

(*Trying to get on the free and easy style again*)

This is quite remarkable, upon my soul! May I ask—

(*Turns toward* HOLMES)

—if it's not an impertinent question, what message you sent up that could have so aroused Miss Faulkner's desire to come down?

HOLMES

(*Looking up at* LARRABEE *innocently*)

Merely that if she wasn't down here in five minutes I'd go up.

LARRABEE

(*Slightly knocked*)

Oh, that was it!

(*Going up into the alcove*)

HOLMES

Quite so.

(*Rises and takes his watch out*)

And unless I'm very much mistaken I hear the young lady on the stairs. In which case she has one and one-half minutes to spare.

(*Moving downstage R.C. by piano—taking opportunity to look at keys, music, etc.*

Enter MADGE LARRABEE *downstairs as if not quite strong, and entering the room L. She has made her face pale, and steadies herself a little by columns, side of arch, furniture, etc. as she comes on, but not overdoing this. She gives the impression of a person a little weak, but endeavoring not to let it be seen*)

LARRABEE

(*L.C. advancing to* MADGE)

Alice—that is, Miss Faulkner, let me introduce Mr. Sherlock Holmes.

(HOLMES *is near piano R.C.* MADGE *goes a step to him with extended hand.* HOLMES *meets* MADGE *near L.C. and takes her hand in the utmost confidence.* LARRABEE *quietly drops down to R.C. going around piano*)

HOLMES

(Meeting MADGE*)*

Miss Faulkner!

MADGE

I'm really most charmed to meet you. Mr. Holmes, I was more than anxious to come down, only the doctor has forbidden my seeing anyone—but when Cousin Freddie said that I might come, of course that placed the responsibility on him, so I have a perfectly clear conscience.

HOLMES

I thank you very much indeed for consenting to see me, Miss Faulkner, I regret that you were put to the trouble of making such a very rapid change of dress.

MADGE

During the day, Mr. Holmes, I am allowed to get up and sit by the window.

HOLMES

Oh, and you were up sitting looking out of the window.

MADGE

Yes.

HOLMES

Admiring the fog?

(She coughs)

MADGE

Mr. Holmes is quite living up to his reputation, isn't he, Freddie?

LARRABEE

I don't know about that.

MADGE

Oh, has he been making mistakes? I'm so sorry!

(*Sits at foot of piano*)

LARRABEE

He's been telling me the most extraordinary things.

MADGE

And they weren't true?

LARRABEE

Well, listen to this one. He wanted to know what there was about the safe in that desk that caused me such anxiety. Ha! Ha! Ha!

MADGE

Why, there isn't anything. Is there?

LARRABEE

That's just it!

(*Swings back the doors of safe*)

There's a perfectly good safe there, but there is nothing in it. Ha! Ha! Ha!

MADGE

(*She laughs*)

My goodness, I wonder what it was Mr. Holmes thought we had in there.

(HOLMES, *seated in armchair L.C. among the cushions, regards* MADGE *and* LARRABEE *with a peculiar, whimsical look*)

LARRABEE

(*Laughing*)

Perhaps you'll do better next time!

(*Closes safe door*)

MADGE

Yes, next time—Mr. Holmes.

(HOLMES *is looking at them*)

You might try on me.

(*Looking playfully at* HOLMES, *as if greatly enjoying the lark*)

LARRABEE

Yes, what do you think of her?

(*Stands at R.*)

HOLMES

It is perfectly easy to discern one thing about Miss Faulkner—and that is, that she is particularly fond of the piano—that her expression wonderful, and her technique extraordinary. While she likes light music well enough, she is also extremely fond of Chopin, Liszt, and Brahms. She plays a great deal indeed; I see it is her chief diversion—which makes it all the more remarkable *that she has not touched the piano for three days.*

MADGE

(*Turning to* LARRABEE—*a trifle disconcerted by* HOLMES'S *last words, but nearly hiding it with success*)

Why, that's quite surprising, isn't it?

LARRABEE

Certainly better than he did for me.

(LARRABEE *remains R. leaning on chair*)

HOLMES

(*Rising*)

I am glad somewhat to repair my shattered reputation, and as a reward will Miss Faulkner play me something of which I am particularly fond.

(*Stands L.*)

MADGE

I shall be delighted—if I can.

> (*Looks questioningly at* HOLMES)

HOLMES

If you can! Something tells me that Chopin's Prelude Number Seven is at your finger ends.

> (LARRABEE *goes down R. with a look of uneasiness*)

MADGE

Oh yes!

> (*Rising and forgetting her illness, and going to key-board—crossing in front of piano*)

I can give you *that*.

HOLMES

> (*Going up L.C.*)

It will please me so much.

MADGE

> (*Stopping suddenly as she is about to sit at piano*)
> (*She coughs*)

Tell me, Mr. Holmes, how did you know so much about my playing—my expression—technique.

HOLMES

> (*Up L.C*)

Miss Faulkner's hands.

MADGE

And my preference for the composers you mentioned?

HOLMES

The music-rack.

MADGE

Oh, how simple! But you mentioned that I hadn't played for three days. How did you . . .

HOLMES

The keys.

MADGE

The keys?

HOLMES

A light layer of dust.

MADGE

Dust! Oh dear!
(Quick business with handkerchief on keyboard)
I never knew Térèse to forget before.
(To HOLMES)
You must think us very untidy, I'm sure, Mr. Holmes.

HOLMES

On the contrary. I infer from many things that you are not untidy in the least, I am therefore compelled to conclude that the failure of Térèse is due to something else.

MADGE

(A little under breath—and hesitatingly—yet compelled by HOLMES's *pointed statement to ask)*
Wh-what?

HOLMES

To some unusual excitement or disturbance that has recently taken place in this house.

MADGE

(*After an instant's pause*)

You're doing very well, Mr. Holmes, and you deserve your Chopin.

(*Sits, makes preparations to play rather hurriedly in order to change the subject*)

HOLMES

(*Up L.C. near bell*)

Thanks.

(LARRABEE *looks toward safe, far from easy in his mind, and leans on R. end of piano, giving* HOLMES *a glance as he turns to* MADGE. MADGE *strikes a few preliminary chords during above business and soon begins to play the composition spoken of. Shortly after the music begins, and while* LARRABEE *is looking to front or elsewhere,* HOLMES *reaches quietly back and pulls the bell crank. No sound of bell heard, the music supposed to make it inaudible. He then sinks into seat just at bell. After a short time* FORMAN *enters up L. and stands waiting just in the archway.* LARRABEE *does not see* FORMAN *at first, but happening to turn discovers him standing there and speaks a warning word to* MADGE *under his breath.* MADGE *hearing* LARRABEE *speak, looks up and sees* FORMAN *L. She stops playing in the midst of a bar—a hesitating stop. Looks at* FORMAN *a moment*)

MADGE

What are you doing here, Judson?

(*Brief pause because* FORMAN *seems surprised*)

FORMAN

I came to see what was wanted, ma'am.

MADGE

What was wanted?

LARRABEE

Nobody asked you to come here.

(*Turning to L.*)

FORMAN

I beg your pardon, sir. I answered the bell.

LARRABEE

(*Becoming savage*)

What bell?

FORMAN

The drawing-room bell, sir.

LARRABEE

(*Threateningly*)

What do you mean, you blockhead?

FORMAN

I'm quite sure it rung, sir.

LARRABEE

(*Loud voice*)

Well, I tell you it did *not* ring!

(*Pause. The* LARRABEES *look angrily at* FORMAN)

HOLMES

(*Seated up L.C. quietly—after slight pause—clear incisive voice*)

Your butler is right, Mr. Chetwood—the bell *did* ring.

(*Brief pause.* LARRABEE *and* MADGE *looking at* HOLMES)

LARRABEE

How do you know?

HOLMES

I rang it.

(MADGE *rises*)

LARRABEE

(*Roughly*)

What do you want?

(HOLMES *rises, takes card from case or pocket*)

HOLMES

I want to send my card to Miss Faulkner.

(*Gives card to* FORMAN.

FORMAN *stands apparently paralyzed*)

LARRABEE

(*Angrily—approaching* HOLMES)

What right have you to ring for servants and give orders in my house?

(MADGE *moves two steps down on R. a little*)

HOLMES

(*Turning on* LARRABEE)

And what right have you to prevent my cards from reaching their destination—and how is it that you and this lady are resorting to trickery and deceit to prevent me from seeing Alice Faulkner?

(*The situation is held an instant and then he turns quietly to* FORMAN)

HOLMES (*Continued*)

Judson, through some trifling oversight, neither of the cards that I handed you has been delivered. See that this *error*—does not occur again.

(FORMAN *stands, apparently uncertain what to do*)

FORMAN

My orders, sir . . .

HOLMES

Oh, you have orders?

FORMAN

I can't say, sir, as I . . .

HOLMES

You were told not to deliver my card!

LARRABEE

And what business is that of yours? I'd like to know?

HOLMES

I shall satisfy your curiosity on that point in a very short time.

LARRABEE

Yes—and you'll find out in a very short time that it isn't safe to meddle with me! It would be no trouble for me to throw you out into the street.

HOLMES

Quite possibly not—but trouble would swiftly follow such an experiment on your part.

LARRABEE

It's a cursed lucky thing for you I'm not armed.

HOLMES

Yes—well, when Miss Faulkner gets down you can go and arm yourself.

LARRABEE

Arm myself! I'll call the police! And what's more I'll do it now.

HOLMES

You will not do it now. You will remain where you are until the young lady I came here to see has entered this room.

LARRABEE

What makes you so sure of that?

HOLMES

Because you will infinitely prefer to avoid an investigation of your very suspicious conduct, Mr. James Larrabee . . . an investigation that shall certainly take place if you or your wife presume further to interfere with my business. As for you, my man—it gives me great pleasure to recall the features of an old acquaintance. Your recent connection with the signing of another man's name to a small piece of paper has made your presence at Bow Street much desired. You will either deliver that card—or you sleep in the police station tonight. It is a matter of small consequence to me which you do.

FORMAN

(*Finally in a low, painful voice—moves to R.C. and whispers hoarsely*)

Shall I go, sir?

(MADGE *moves to near* LARRABEE, *R.C., at piano*)

LARRABEE

Yes, go on. Take it up—it can make no difference to me.

MADGE

(*Quick, sharp aside to* LARRABEE)

Yes, but if she comes down, can't he get the letters away from her?

LARRABEE

(*To* MADGE)

If he does, Sid Prince is waiting for him outside.

HOLMES

(*On seeing* ALICE *rises and puts book on mantel. After a brief pause, turns and comes down to* LARRABEE)

A short while since you displayed an acute anxiety to leave the room. Pray do not let me detain you or your wife—any longer.

(*The* LARRABEES *do not move—they are turned away at R. After brief pause,* HOLMES *shrugs shoulders slightly and goes over L.C. to* ALICE. HOLMES *and* ALICE *regard each other a moment*)

ALICE

This is Mr. Holmes?

HOLMES

Yes.

ALICE

You wished to see me?

HOLMES

Very much indeed, Miss Faulkner, but I am sorry to see—

(*Placing chair near her*)

—you are far from well.

(ALICE *comes L.C. a step.* LARRABEE *gives a quick glance across at her threateningly and a gesture of warning, but keeping it down*)

ALICE

Oh no—

(*Stops as she catches* LARRABEE's *angry glance from R.*)

HOLMES

(*Pausing as he is about to place chair and looking at her*)

No?

(Lets go of his chair)

I beg your pardon—but—

(Goes to her and takes her hand delicately—looks at red marks on her wrist. Looking up at her)

What does that mean?

ALICE

(Shrinking a little. Sees LARRABEE'S *cruel glance from R.)*

Oh—nothing.

*(*HOLMES *looks steadily at her an instant)*

HOLMES

Nothing!

ALICE

(Shaking head)

No!

HOLMES

And the—

(Pointing lightly)

—mark here on your neck plainly showing the clutch of a man's fingers?

(Indicating a place on her neck where more marks appear)

Do they mean nothing also?

(Pause. ALICE *turns slightly away without answering.*

Looking straight before him to front)

It occurs to me that I would like to have an explanation of this . . . Possibly—

(Turns slowly toward LARRABEE)

—you can furnish one, Mr. Larrabee?

(Pause)

LARRABEE

(*Doggedly*)

How should I know?

HOLMES

It seems to have happened in your house.

LARRABEE

(*Advancing a little R.C. becoming violently angry*)

What if it did? You'd better understand that it isn't healthy for you or anyone else to interfere with my business.

HOLMES

(*Quickly—incisively*)

Ah! Then it is your business. We have that much at least.

(LARRABEE *stops suddenly and holds himself in.*

Turning to ALICE)

Pray be seated, Miss Faulkner.

(*Placing chair as if not near enough.*

ALICE *hesitates an instant—then decides to remain standing for the present.* LARRABEE *moves up near L. end of piano and stands watching and listening to interview between* HOLMES *and* ALICE)

ALICE

I don't know who you are, Mr. Holmes, or why you are here.

HOLMES

I shall be very glad to answer that question. As far as my identity is concerned, you have my name and address as well as the announcement of my profession inscribed upon the card, which I observe you still hold clasped tightly in the fingers of your left hand.

(ALICE *at once looks at the card in her hand*)

ALICE

(*A look at him*)

A—detective!

(*Sits on ottoman L. looking at* HOLMES)

HOLMES

(*Draws chair near her and sits*)

Quite so. And my business is this. I have been consulted as to the possibility of obtaining from you certain letters and other things which are supposed to be in your possession, and which—I need not tell you—are the source of the great anxiety.

ALICE

(*Her manner changing and no longer timid and shrinking*)

It is quite true that I have such letters, Mr. Holmes, but it would be impossible to get them from me; others—

(*A very slight look to R.*)

—have tried—and failed.

HOLMES

What others have or have not done, whilst possibly instructive in certain directions, can in no way affect my conduct. I have come to you frankly and directly, to beg you to pity and forgive.

ALICE

There are some things, Mr. Holmes, beyond pity—beyond forgiveness.

HOLMES

But there are others that are not.

(ALICE *looks at him*)

HOLMES (*Continued*)

I am able to assure you of the sincere penitence—the deep regret
—of the one who inflicted the injury, and of his earnest desire to
make—any reparation in his power.

ALICE

How can reparation be made to the dead?

HOLMES

How indeed! And by the very same token any injury you may
yourself be able to inflict by means of these things can be no
reparation—no satisfaction—no indemnity to the one no longer
here. You will be acting for the *living*—not the dead. For your
own satisfaction, Miss Faulkner, your own gratification and your
own revenge!

(ALICE *starts slightly at the idea suggested and rises.
Pause.* HOLMES *rises, moves his chair back a little,
standing with his hand on it*)

ALICE

(*Stands a moment, very quiet, low voice*)

I know—from this—and from other things that have happened
that a marriage is—contemplated.

HOLMES

That is quite true.

ALICE

I *cannot* give up what I intend to do, Mr. Holmes. There are
other things beside revenge—there is punishment. If I am not
able to communicate with the family to which this man proposes
to ally himself—in time to prevent such a thing—the punishment will come later—but you may be perfectly sure it will
come.

(HOLMES *is about to speak. She motions him not to speak*)

There is nothing more to say!

(HOLMES *gives a signal*)

Good night, Mr. Holmes.

(*She looks at* HOLMES *an instant. She turns and goes up L.*)

HOLMES

But, my dear Miss Faulkner, before you—

(*A confused noise of shouting and terrified screams from below, followed by sounds of people running up a stairway and through the halls.*

Goes up R.C. ALICE *hearing noise, stops down L.C.*)

TÉRÈSE

(*Off stage*)

Au secours, mon Dieu, au secours.

(ALL *stop and listen. Noise louder. Enter* FORMAN *up L., breathless and white. At same time smoke pours in through archway up L.*)

FORMAN

(*Gasping*)

Mr. Chetwood! Mr. Chetwood!

MADGE and LARRABEE

(*Moving across toward L.*)

What is it?

(HOLMES *moves quietly up R. of piano, keeping his eyes sharply on* ALICE. ALICE *stands back L.C. alarmed*)

The lamp—in the kitchen, sir! It fell off the table—an' everything down there is blazin', sir.

(*Pause for* ALICE's *business as detailed below*)

MADGE

The house—is on fire! Térèse, keep calm, keep calm, Térèse.

(*She gives a glance toward safe, forgetting that the package is gone—but instantly recovers and hurries toward L.*

LARRABEE *hurriedly exits up* L. MADGE *after him.* FORMAN *disappears up* L. *Noise of people running downstairs, etc.* ALICE, *on cue "Blazin', sir," gives a scream and looks quickly at chair up* C. *at the same time making an involuntary start toward it. She stops upon seeing* HOLMES *and stands. Noises grow less and die away outside L. and below*)

HOLMES

(*Up C.*)

Don't alarm yourself, Miss Faulkner—

(*Slight shake of head*)

—there is no fire.

ALICE

(*A step back to L.—shows by tones that she fears something*)

No fire!

(*Stands dreading what may come*)

HOLMES

The smoke was all arranged for by me.

(*Slight pause*)

ALICE

Arranged for?

(*Looks at* HOLMES.

HOLMES *moves to large upholstered chair quickly which* ALICE *glanced at and made start toward a moment since*)

What does this mean, Mr. Holmes?

> (HOLMES *feels rapidly over chair. Rips away uphol-*
> *stery.* ALICE *attempts to stop him—goes up C., but is*
> *too late, and backs to piano R.C., almost in a fainting*
> *condition.* HOLMES *stands erect with a package in his*
> *hand*)

HOLMES

That I wanted this package of letters, Miss Faulkner—

> (ALICE *stands looking at* HOLMES *speechless—motion-*
> *less—meets* HOLMES's *gaze for a moment and then cov-*
> *ers her face with her hands, and very slight motion of*
> *convulsive sob or two.* HOLMES *with a quick motion*
> *steps quickly in a businesslike way to the seat which his*
> *coat, hat, and cane are, and picks up coat, throwing it*
> *over his arm as if to go at once*)

HOLMES (*Continued*)

(*Low voice. Brief pause*)

I will not take them, Miss Faulkner.

> (*He looks down an instant. Her eyes are upon his face*
> *steadily*)

As you—

> (*Still looking down*)

—very likely conjecture, the—alarm of fire was only to make you betray their hiding place—and as you saw I—availed myself of that betrayal—. But now that I witness your great distress—I find I cannot take them—unless—

> (*Looking at her*)

—you can possibly—change your mind and let me have them— of your own free will . . .

> (*He looks at her a moment. She shakes her head very*
> *slightly*)

I hardly supposed you could.

(Looks down a moment. Looks up)

I shall therefore—

(Very slight pause, and he is about to start toward her as if to hand her the package.

Sound of quick footsteps outside L. Enter LARRABEE *up L., with a revolver in his hand, followed by* MADGE, *who goes down L. behind* LARRABEE.

Stop music)

LARRABEE

So. You've got them, have you? And now, I suppose we're going to see you walk out of the house with them.

(Handles revolver with meaning.

HOLMES *looks quietly at* LARRABEE *an instant.* MADGE *stands down L.)*

HOLMES

On the contrary, you're going to see me return them to their rightful owner.

LARRABEE

(With revolver)

Yes—I think that'll be the safest thing for Mr. Sherlock Holmes to do.

*(HOLMES *stops dead and looks at* LARRABEE *and walks quietly down facing him)*

HOLMES

You flatter yourself, Mr. Larrabee. The reason that I do not leave the house with this package of papers is not because of you or what you may do—or say—or think—or feel! It is solely on account of this young lady!

(To ALICE)

It is a matter of constant regret, Miss Faulkner, that my chosen profession involves me with an underworld most of whose members are not gentlemen. But although Mr. Larrabee may not understand honor, I feel sure that you do. Allow me to place this in your hands.

(*Gives her package*)

Should you ever be so generous, so forgiving, as to wish to return them to the one who wrote them, you have my address. In any event, rest assured that there will be no more cruelty, no more persecution in this house. You are perfectly safe with your property now—for I have so arranged it that your faintest cry of distress will be heard! Good night, Miss Faulkner.

(*Pause—turns to* LARRABEE *and* MADGE. *Coming to them*)

As for you, sir, and you, madam, I beg you to understand that you continue your persecution of that young lady *at your peril.*

(ALICE *looks at* HOLMES *an instant, uncertain what to do. He makes a slight motion indictating her to go.* ALICE, *after slight pause, crosses in front of* HOLMES *and exits up L.* LARRABEE *makes slight move toward* ALICE, *but is checked by a look from* HOLMES. HOLMES *waits, exit. Then he looks after her for a moment. Then turns and takes his coat and hat. Looks at them an instant*)

HOLMES

Oh, good evening—

(*Walks out up L., and the sound of heavy door closing is heard outside L.*

Pause. LARRABEE *and* MADGE *stand where* HOLMES *left them. Sound of window R. opening.* SID PRINCE *hurries in at window up R.*)

PRINCE

(*Sharp but subdued up R.*)

Well! 'E didn't get the stuff, did 'e?

(LARRABEE *shakes head and moves to R.C. below piano.* PRINCE *looks at him, puzzled, and then turns toward* MADGE, *who comes C.*)

MADGE

He gave it to *her*.

(*L.C.*)

PRINCE

(*C.*)

What!—'e found it? An' gave it to the girl?

(MADGE *repeats slight affirmative motion*)

Well 'ere—I say! Wot are you waiting for, Now's the chance—before she 'ides it again!

(*Starting as if to go L.*)

MADGE

(*Stopping* PRINCE *up L.C.*)

No! Wait!

(*Glances around nervously*)

PRINCE

Wot's the matter!

(*Going R.C. to* LARRABEE)

Do you want to lose it?

LARRABEE

(*R. sudden turn*)

No! You're right! It's all a cursed bluff!

(*Starting as if to go L.*)

MADGE

(*Meeting them near C. as if to stop them*)

No, no, Jim!

LARRABEE

I tell you we will! Now's our chance to get a-hold of it!

(*Going L. Pushing her aside upstage*)

PRINCE

(*Going L.*)

Well, I should say so!

(*Three knocks are heard just as* PRINCE *and* LARRABEE *reach archway. A distant sound of three heavy blows as if struck from underneath up against the floor, reverberates through the house.* ALL *stop motionless.*
Pause.
Music, melodramatic agitato, very soft, till Curtain*)

LARRABEE

(*In a low voice*)

What's that?

MADGE

Someone at the door.

(PRINCE *crosses to up R., indicating up stage, then glances around alarmed.* MADGE *rings bell up C.* LARRABEE *crosses slowly to R.C. Enter* FORMAN *at door up C. All stand easily as if nothing out of the usual*)

MADGE

I think someone knocked, Judson.

(FORMAN *at once goes quietly but quickly to L., and exits L. Sound of door outside L. closing again.* FORMAN *re-enters L.*)

FORMAN

I beg pardon, ma'am, there's no one at the door.

MADGE

That's all, Judson.

(*Exit* FORMAN *L.*)

PRINCE

(*Speaks almost in a whisper from above piano*)

'E's got us watched! Wot we want to do is to leave it alone an' let the Hemperor 'ave it!

MADGE

(*Low voice—taking a step or two toward* PRINCE *up R.C.*)

Do you mean—Professor Moriarty?

(LARRABEE *down R.C. turns to* PRINCE)

PRINCE

That's 'oo I mean. Once let 'im get at it and 'e'll settle it with 'Olmes pretty quick.

(*Turns to* LARRABEE)

Meet me at Leary's—nine sharp—in the morning.

(*Looks L., and upstage R. quickly. Goes up R. and turns to them again*)

Don't you worry! I tell you the Professor'll get 'im before tomorrow night! 'E don't wait long either! An' w'en he strikes—it means death.

(*Exit at window up R.*

Brief pause. After PRINCE *exits,* MADGE *moves to R., and looks after him from above piano.* LARRABEE *crosses slowly toward L. When he is about C., he stops suddenly with a despairing look on his face, leans on chair—looks around puzzled. His eyes meet* MADGE's *as LIGHTS FADE away*)

CURTAIN

Scene 2

This scene is built inside the second. PROFESSOR
MORIARTY's *underground office. A large, vaultlike
room, with rough masonry walls and vaulted ceiling.
The general idea of this place is that it has been con-
verted from a cellar room of a warehouse into a fairly
comfortable office or headquarters. There are no windows.*

*The color or tone of this set must not be similar to
the Second Act set, which is a gloomy and dark bluish-
brown. The effect in this set should be of masonry that
has long ago been whitewashed and is now old,
stained, and grimy. Maps on wall of England, France,
Germany, Russia, etc. Also a marked map of London
—heavy spots upon certain localities. Many charts of
buildings, plans of floors—possible tunnelings, etc.
Many books about—on impoverished shelves, etc.*

PROFESSOR ROBERT MORIARTY *is seated at a large circular desk up R. facing the front. He is looking over
letters, telegrams, papers, etc., as if morning mail. He
is a middle-aged man, with massive head and gray
hair, and a face full of character, overhanging brow,
heavy jaw . . . a man of great intellectual force, extremely tall and thin. His forehead domes out in a white
curve, and his two eyes are deeply sunken in his head.
Clean-shaven, pale, ascetic-looking. Shoulders rounded
and face protruding forward, and forever oscillating
from side to side in a curiously reptilian fashion. Deep,
hollow voice.*

The room is dark, with light showing on his face, as if from a lamp. Pause. He picks up a speaking tube and puts it to his mouth.

JOHN

Yes, sir?

MORIARTY

(*Speaking into tube in a low voice*)
Has any report come in from Chibley?

JOHN

Nothing yet, sir.

MORIARTY

Send Bassick.
> (*Tube down. Buzzer outside door rings twice.*
> MORIARTY *picks up tube and speaks into it*)

JOHN

John here. Send Bassick.

MORIARTY

(*Speaking into tube*)
Number.
> (*Listens. Speaks into tube again*)

Correct.
> (*He slides back bolt of door.*
> *Enter* BASSICK *noiselessly. Bolt of door slides back.*
> BASSICK *goes to* MORIARTY's *desk at once and stands.*
> MORIARTY *motions him to sit. He does*)

Now . . . before we go into anything else, I want to refer to Davidson.

BASSICK

I've made a note of him myself, sir; he's holding back money.

MORIARTY

Something like six hundred short on that last haul, isn't it?

BASSICK

Certainly as much as that.

MORIARTY

Have him attended to. Craigin is the one to do it.

(BASSICK *writes memo quickly*)

And see that his disappearance is noticed. Have it spoken of . . .
That finishes Davidson. Now as to this Blaisdale matter—did
you learn anything more?

BASSICK

The whole thing was a trap.

MORIARTY

What do you mean?

BASSICK

A trap set and baited by an expert.

MORIARTY

But those letters and papers of instructions—you brought them
back, or destroyed them, I trust?

BASSICK

No, I could not do it, sir—Manning had disappeared and the
papers are gone.

(*Music melodramatic. Cue, as* MORIARTY *looks at*
BASSICK)

MORIARTY

Gone! Holmes again. That's bad for the Underwood trial.

BASSICK

But, I thought Shakleford was going to get a postponement.

MORIARTY

He tried to—and found he was blocked.

BASSICK

Who could have done it?

(MORIARTY *turns and looks at* BASSICK *almost hypnotically—his head vibrating from side to side as if making him speak the name*)

Sherlock Holmes?

MORIARTY

Holmes, Holmes, Holmes!

(*His eyes still on* BASSICK. BASSICK *as if fascinated by* MORIARTY. *Slight affirmative motion*)

He's got hold of thirty papers and instructions in as many jobs, some as to putting a man or two out of the way. And he's gradually completing chains of evidence which, if we let him go on will reach to me as sure as the sun will rise. Reach to me! He's playing rather a dangerous game! Inspector Wilson tried it seven years ago. Wilson is dead. Two years Henderson took it up. We haven't heard very much of Henderson, lately, eh?

BASSICK

Not a thing, sir!

MORIARTY

He's rather a talented man. This Holmes, he hopes to drag me in at the Underwood trial, but he doesn't realize what can happen between now and Monday. There isn't a street in London that'll be safe for him if I whisper his name to Craigin—I might even pay him a little call myself—just for the satisfaction of it. Baker Street, isn't it? His place?

BASSICK

Baker Street, sir.

MORIARTY

We could make it absolutely secure for three streets each way.

BASSICK

Yes, sir, but—

MORIARTY

We could. We've done it elsewhere over and over again—police decoyed. Men in every doorway. Do this tonight—in Baker Street! At nine o'clock call his attendants out on some pretext or other, and keep them out, you understand? I'll see this Holmes myself—I'll give him a chance for his life. If he declines to treat with me—Holmes and I have been fencing for years. A hint there, a note here. The average inspector's only a generation away from a line of bumpkins stretching back into oblivion, but this Holmes . . . Over the years the pond gets smaller and smaller; we grow together like a couple of greedy old pike. Either I eat him or he eats me, or we choke on each other. But either way, one of us must go. They'll find his body washed up on the Isle of Dogs and conclude it was a thick dark night and that he slipped on Waterloo Bridge with its low parapet and once he's dead they'll never find me: they'll never know.

> (*He takes a savage-looking bulldog revolver from under desk and examines it carefully, slowly placing it in breast pocket. Ring of a telephone bell is heard, but not until the revolver business is finished.*
>
> MORIARTY *gives a nod to* BASSICK, *indicating him to attend to the phone.* BASSICK *rises and goes to and picks up telephone.* MORIARTY *resumes business of examining papers on desk*)

BASSICK

(*Speaks into receiver*)

Yes—yes—Bassick. What name did you say? Oh, Prince, yes. He'll have to wait—yes—I got his telegram last night— Well, tell him to come and speak to me at the phone . . . Yes—I got your telegram, Prince, but I have an important matter on. You'll have to wait—who? Sherlock Holmes? Fighting against you in some job. What sort of a game is it?— Where is he now? Wait a moment.

MORIARTY

(*Quickly turning to* BASSICK)

Well, ask him what it is.

(BASSICK *is about to speak through telephone*)

BASSICK

Prince . . .

MORIARTY

No, wait! Send him here.

(BASSICK *turns in surprise*)

BASSICK

But, no one sees you, sir. No one knows you. That has meant safety for years.

MORIARTY

No one sees me now. You will talk with him—I'll be there. This is *your office*— you understand—*your office*—I'll be there.

(BASSICK *turns to telephone*)

BASSICK

Is that you, Prince? Yes, I find I can't come out—but I'll see you here— What interest have they got? What's the name?

(*To* MORIARTY)

He says there's two with him—a man and a woman named Larrabee. They won't consent to any interview unless they're present.

MORIARTY

Send them in.

BASSICK

Eh, Prince? Ask John to come to the telephone—oh, John—

(*Lower voice*)

Those people with Prince, do they seem to be all right? Look close—yes?—well, take them out through the warehouse and down by the circular stairway and then bring them here by the long tunnel—yes, here—look them over as you go along to see if they're carrying anything—and watch that no one sees you come down—yes.

(*Hangs up*)

I don't like this, sir.

MORIARTY

You lack stature, Bassick.

(*Buzzer sounds*)

MORIARTY (*Continued*)

Your office, remember. Your office.

BASSICK

(*Takes tube and speaks*)

Number . . . are the three waiting with you?

(*Listens—drops tube and pushes lever back, and the bolt slides back from the door. Door swings open. Enter* SID PRINCE, MADGE, *and* LARRABEE
BASSICK *sits behind desk*)

BASSICK

I understand you to say, through our private telephone—that you've got something with Sherlock Holmes against you.

PRINCE

Yes, sir—we 'ave.

BASSICK

Kindly let me have the particulars.

PRINCE

Jim and Madge Larrabee here, have picked up a girl in 'Omburg where her sister had been havin' a strong affair of the heart with a very 'igh young foreign nobs who promised to marry 'er—but the family stepped in and threw the whole thing down. 'E'd be'aved very bad an' had let 'imself out an' written her letters an' given her rings and tokens, yer see—and there was photographs too. Now, as these various things showed how 'e'd deceived and betrayed 'er, they wouldn't look very nice at all considerin' who the young man was, an' wot 'igh titles he was comin' into. So when this girl up and dies of it all, these letters and things all fall into the 'ands of the sister—which is the one my friends Jim and Madge, Madge and Jim 'ere has been nursin' all along.

BASSICK

(*To* LARRABEE)

Where have you kept her?

LARRABEE

We took a house up the Norrington Road.

BASSICK

How long have you been there?

LARRABEE

Two years, the fourteenth of next month.

BASSICK

And those letters and—other evidences of the young man's misconduct—when will they reach their full value?

(LARRABEE *is about to answer, but* PRINCE *jumps in quickly*)

PRINCE

It's now, don't you see. It's now—there's a marriage comin' on an' there's been offers, an' the problem is to get the papers in our 'ands.

BASSICK

Where are they?

PRINCE

Why, the girl's got 'old of 'em, sir!

(BASSICK *turns for explanation of this to* LARRABEE)

LARRABEE

We had a safe for her to keep them in, supposing that when the time came we could open it, but the lock was out of order so we got Prince in to help us. He opened it last night and the package containing the things was gone.

PRINCE

Gone?

BASSICK

Gone? What did you do when you discovered this?

PRINCE

Do—I 'adn't any more than got the safe open, sir, an' given one look at it, when Sherlock Holmes rings the front-door bell.

BASSICK

(*Intent*)

There—at your house?

LARRABEE

At my house.

BASSICK

He didn't get those letters?

LARRABEE

Well, he did get them, but he passed them back to the Faulkner girl.

BASSICK

(*Rises—in surprise*)

Passed them back, eh? What did that mean?

(*Goes down R. a little, thinking*)

LARRABEE

(*Slight shrug of shoulders*)

And there's another thing that puzzles me. There was an accident below in the kitchen—a lamp fell off the table scattering burning oil about, the butler ran up, yelling fire. We ran down there, and a few buckets of water put it out.

(MORIARTY *suddenly appears at his desk up R.C. Lights on his face*)

MORIARTY

I have a suggestion to make.

(ALL *turn in surprise and look at* MORIARTY)

The first thing we must do is to get rid of your butler—not discharge him—*get rid of him.*

(*To* BASSICK)

Craigin for that! Today! As soon as it's dark. Give him two others to help—Mr. Larrabee will send the man into the cellar for something—they'll be waiting for him there. Doulton's van will get the body to the river.

(MADGE *shudders slightly*)

It need not inconvenience you at all, madam, we do these things quietly.

> (BASSICK *is writing orders at R.*
>
> *To* BASSICK)

Bassick, what's the Seraph doing?

BASSICK

He's on the Reading job tomorrow night.

MORIARTY

Put him with Craigin today to help with that butler. But there's something else we want. Now have you seen those letters, the photographs, and whatever else there may be? Have you seen them? Do you know what they're like?

MADGE

I have. I've looked them through carefully several times.

MORIARTY

Now could you make me a counterfeit set of those things and tie them up so that they will look exactly like the package Sherlock Holmes held in his hand last night?

MADGE

I could manage the letters—but—

MORIARTY

You manage the letters, I'll send someone else to manage the rest —from your description. Bassick—that old German artist.

BASSICK

Leuftner.

MORIARTY

Precisely, Leuftner. Send Leuftner to Mrs. Larrabee at eleven.

> (*Looks at watch*)

It's now a quarter past ten—that gives you three quarters of an hour to reach home. I shall want the counterfeit at eleven tonight—twelve hours to make it.

MADGE

It will be ready, sir.

MORIARTY

Good! Bassick—notify the Lascar that I may require the gas chamber at Stepney tonight.

BASSICK

Gas chamber!

MORIARTY

Yes, The one that backs over the river—and have Craigin there a quarter before twelve with two others. Mr. Larrabee—
  (*Turns slightly to him*)
I shall want you to write a letter to Mr. Sherlock Holmes which I shall dictate—and tonight I may require a little assistance from you both.
  (*Taking in* PRINCE *with his glance*)
Meet me here at eleven.

LARRABEE

This is all very well, sir, but you have said nothing yet about—the business arrangements. I'm not sure that I—

MORIARTY

  (*Turning front*)
You have no choice.

LARRABEE

No choice.
  (*Looks fiercely to* MORIARTY.

MADGE *rises to quiet him.* JOHN *drops handkerchief.*
Pause)

MORIARTY

(*Looking at him.*)

No choice.

(PRINCE *aghast*)

MORIARTY (*Continued*)

I do what I please. It pleases me to take hold of this case.

LARRABEE

(*Angry—crossing to desk up R.C.*)

And, what about pleasing me?

(BASSICK *moves at R. of* MORIARTY *and looks across at*
LARRABEE)

MORIARTY

(*Perfectly quiet—looks at* LARRABEE *an instant*)

I am not so sure but I shall be able to do that as well. I will obtain the original letters from Miss Faulkner and negotiate them
for far more than you could possibly obtain. In addition—you
will have an opportunity tonight to sell the counterfeit package
to Mr. Sherlock Holmes for a good round sum. And the money
obtained from both these sources shall be divided as follows: you
will take one hundred per cent and I—nothing.

(*Brief pause of astonishment*)

LARRABEE

Nothing!

MORIARTY

Nothing!

(LARRABEE *moves L. to* PRINCE)

BASSICK

(*On* MORIARTY'*s R.*)

But we cannot negotiate those letters until we know who they incriminate. Mr. Larrabee has not yet informed us.

MORIARTY

Mr. Larrabee—

(LARRABEE *looks around to* MORIARTY)

—is wise in exercising caution. He values the keystone to his arch. But he will consent to let me know.

(LARRABEE *goes to* MADGE)

MADGE

(*Going across to* MORIARTY)

Professor Moriarty, that information we would like to give—only to you.

(*Looking toward* BASSICK.

MORIARTY *motions* BASSICK *away.* BASSICK *moves away.* BASSICK *moves down R. a little.* MORIARTY *hands a card and pencil to* MADGE *from desk.* MADGE *writes a name and hands it to* MORIARTY. *He glances at name on card, then looks more closely. Looks up at* MADGE, *astonished.*)

MORIARTY

This is an absolute certainty.

LARRABEE

Absolute.

MORIARTY

It means that you have a fortune.

(PRINCE *drinks in every word and look*)

Had I known this, you should hardly have had such terms.

LARRABEE

Oh well—we don't object to a—

MORIARTY

(*Interrupting*)

The arrangement is made. I bid you good morning, Mr. Larrabee.

(*Bowing with dignity and pulling lever back.*

LARRABEE, PRINCE, *and* MADGE *move toward door. Bolts, etc., slide back on door.* BASSICK *motions* JOHN, *who stands ready to conduct the party.* BASSICK *crosses to door. All bow a little and exit, followed by* JOHN—*business of door closing, bolts, etc.* BASSICK *turns at door and looks at* MORIARTY)

Bassick, place your men at nine tonight for Sherlock Holmes's house in Baker Street.

BASSICK

You will go there *yourself*, sir?

MORIARTY

I will go there *myself*—I'll offer him peace or death.

BASSICK

But this meeting tonight at twelve, to trap Holmes in the gas chamber in Swandem Lane.

MORIARTY

If I fail in Baker Street, we'll trap him tonight in Swandem Lane. Either way I have him, I have him.

(*Lights off gradually but not too slow on this act, and leave light on* MORIARTY'S *face last. Music. Swell out forte for change. DARK CHANGE*)

Scene 3

In SHERLOCK HOLMES's *rooms in Baker Street—the large drawing room of his apartments. An open, cheerful room, but not too much decorated. Rather plain. The walls are a plain tint, the ceiling ditto. The furniture is comfortable and good, but not elegant. Books, music, violins, tobacco pouches, pipes, tobacco, etc., are scattered in places about the room with some disorder. Various odd things are hung about. Some very choice pictures and etchings hang on the walls here and there, but the pictures do not have heavy gilt frames. All rather simple. The room gives more an impression of an artist's studio. A wide door up right side to hall (and thus by stairway to street door). Door up L. communicating with bedroom or dining room. A fireplace down or half-down L. side with cheerful grate fire burning, throwing a red glow into room. Through a large arch, up L.C., can be seen a laboratory and a table with chemicals and various knickknacks. Furniture according to the scene plot. The lighting should be arranged so that after the dark change the first thing that becomes visible—even before the rest of the room—is the glow of the fire, the blue flame of the spirit lamp—and* SHERLOCK HOLMES *seated among cushions on the floor before the fire. Light gradually on, but still leaving the effect of only firelight.*

Music stops, just as LIGHTS UP.

SHERLOCK HOLMES *is discovered on the floor before the fire. He is in a dressing gown and slippers and has his pipe.* HOLMES *leans against the Chesterfield. A violin is upon the Chesterfield, and the bow near it, as if recently laid down. Other things scattered about him. He sits smoking a while, in deep thought. Bell rings off R. Enter* BILLY, *the boy page, or buttons, at door up R. He comes down to back of table.*

BILLY

It's Dr. Watson, sir. You told me as I could always show him up.

HOLMES

Well, I should think so.

(*Enter* WATSON)

Ah, Watson, my dear fellow.

WATSON

How are you, Holmes?

HOLMES

Perfectly delighted to see you, my dear fellow, perfectly delighted. Wedlock suits you, Watson. You have put on seven and one-half pounds since I saw you.

WATSON

Seven pounds actually.

HOLMES

Indeed I should have thought a little more. Just a trifle more, I fancy. But I also infer that you are in danger of losing it again if your wife remains away from home much longer.

WATSON

Indeed she returns tomorrow from a little visit. But how do you know?

HOLMES

How did I know? I observed it. How do I know that you have opened a consulting room and resumed the practice of medicine without letting me hear a word about it? How do I know that you've been getting your feet very wet lately, that you have engaged a most clumsy and careless servant girl—and that you've moved your dressing table to the other side of your room?

WATSON

My dear Holmes, if you lived a few centuries ago, they would have burned you alive.

HOLMES

Whereas you, my dear Doctor, would be as safe as house in any century you chose. Lucky man.

WATSON

Tell me, how did you know all that?

HOLMES

It is simplicity itself. There are scratches and parallel cuts on your right boot, there where the firelight strikes it. Somebody scraped away crusted mud and did it badly. There's your wet feet and careless servant girl all on one foot. Your face is badly shaved on your right side—you always used to be badly shaved on your left side—you couldn't very well move your window— you must have moved your dressing table.

WATSON

By Jove, yes! But my medical practice—I fail to see how you worked that out.

HOLMES

My dear Watson, if a gentleman walks into my room reeking of iodoform, and with a black mark of nitrate of silver on the inner side of his right forefinger, the characteristic tiny bulge in his top hat where he normally secrets his stethoscope, I must be dull indeed if I do not pronounce him to be an active member of the medical profession.

WATSON

Ha! Ha! Of course. But how the deuce did you know my wife was away?

HOLMES

Where the deuce is your second waistcoat button, and what the deuce is yesterday's carnation doing in today's lapel? This is elementary! Child's play of deduction.

(HOLMES *moves to the mantel, reaches, removes hypodermic syringe, carefully adjusting the needle. Fills from phial. Then rolls back left cuff of shirt a little. Pause, looks at arm or wrist a moment. Inserts needle. Presses piston home.*

Music. A weird bar or two—keeping on a strange pulsation on one note for cocaine business. Begin as HOLMES *fills syringe.*

WATSON *has watched him with an expression of deep anxiety, but with effort to restrain himself from speaking*)

WATSON

(*As* HOLMES *puts needle in case again. Finally speaks*)
Which is it today? Cocaine or morphine or—

HOLMES

Cocaine, my dear fellow. A seven per cent solution. I'm back to my old love. (*Offering syringe and phial.*) Would you like to try some?

WATSON

(*Emphatically—rises*)
Certainly *not*.

HOLMES

(*As if surprised*)

Oh! I'm sorry!

WATSON

I have no wish to break *my* system down before it's time.

(*Pause*)

HOLMES

Quite right, my dear Doctor—quite right—but, you see, my time has come.

(*Goes to mantel and replaces case thereon. Throws himself languidly into Chesterfield and leans back in luxurious enjoyment of the drug*)

WATSON

(*Goes to table, resting hand on upper corner, looking at* HOLMES *seriously*)

Holmes, for months I've seen you using these deadly drugs—in ever-increasing doses. When they lay hold of you there is no end. It must go on, and on—until the finish.

HOLMES

(*Lying back dreamily*)

So must you go on and on, eating your breakfast—until the finish.

WATSON

(*Approaching* HOLMES)

Breakfast is food. These drugs are poisons—slow but certain. They involve tissue changes of a most *serious* nature.

HOLMES

Just what I want. I'm bored to death with my old tissues. I want to get a whole new lot in.

WATSON

(*Going near* HOLMES—*putting hand on* HOLMES's *shoulder*)

Ah, really, Holmes—I'm trying to save you.

HOLMES

(*Earnest at once—places right hand on* WATSON's *arm*)

Well, you can't do it, old fellow—so don't waste your time.

(*Music stops.*

They look at one another an instant. WATSON *sees cigarette on table—picks it up and sits in chair R. of table, facing front*)

Watson, to change the subject a little. In the enthusiasm which has prompted you to chronicle and—if you will excuse my saying so somewhat to embellish—a few of my little—adventures, you have occasionally committed the error—or indiscretion—of giving to them a certain tinge of romance which struck me as being a trifle out of place. Something like working an elopement into the fifth proposition of Euclid. I merely refer to this in case you should see fit at some future time—to chronicle the most important and far-reaching case of my career—one upon which I have labored for fourteen months, and which is rapidly approaching a singularly diverting climax—I allude to the case of Professor Moriarty.

WATSON

Moriarty! I don't remember ever having heard of the fellow.

HOLMES

The Napoleon of crime. Watson! He sits motionless like an ugly, venomous spider in the center of his web—but that web has ten thousand radiations and that spider knows every quiver of every one of them.

WATSON

Really! This is very interesting.

HOLMES

Ah—but my dear Doctor, the real interest will come when the professor begins to realize his position—which he cannot fail to do shortly. By ten o'clock tomorrow night the time will be ripe for the arrests. Then the greatest criminal trial of the century . . . the clearing up of over forty mysteries . . . and the rope for everyone.

WATSON

Good! But what will he do when he sees that you have him?

HOLMES

Do? He will do me the honor, my dear Doctor, of bending every resource of his wonderful organization of criminals to the one purpose of my destruction.

WATSON

Why, Holmes, this is a dangerous thing.

    (*Rises*)

HOLMES

On the contrary, it's perfectly delightful! It saves me innumerable doses of those deadly drugs upon which you occasionally favor me with your medical views! Watson, my whole life is a series of frantic endeavors to escape the commonplace of existence! For a brief moment I escape! You should congratulate me!

WATSON

    (*Crosses over to R.*)

But you could escape them without such serious risks! Your other cases have not been so dangerous, and they were even more interesting.

(*Gets back to table below chair*)

Now, the one you spoke of—the last time I saw you—the recovery of those damaging letters and gifts from a young girl—

(HOLMES *suddenly rises—stands motionless.* WATSON *looks at him surprised. Brief pause. Then* WATSON *sits in armchair R.C.*)

Oh, it was a most peculiar affair, as I remember it. You were going to try the experiment of making her betray their hiding place by an alarm of fire in her own home—and after that—

HOLMES

—after that.

(*Pause*)

WATSON

Didn't the plan succeed?

HOLMES

Of course—as far as I've gone.

WATSON

You got Forman into the house as butler?

HOLMES

(*Nods*)

Forman was in as butler.

WATSON

And upon your signal he overturned a lamp in the kitchen—

(HOLMES *moves up L. and down*)

—scattered the smoke balls and gave an alarm of fire?

(HOLMES *nods and mutters "Yes" under his breath*)

And the young lady—did she—

HOLMES

(*Turning and interrupting*)

She did. It all transpired precisely as planned. I took the packet of papers from its hiding place—and as I told you I would, I handed it back to Miss Faulkner.

WATSON

But you never told me *why* you proposed to hand it back.

HOLMES

(*Standing just above table*)

For a very simple reason, my dear Doctor. That it would have been theft for me to take it. The contents of the packet are absolutely the property of the young lady.

WATSON

Yes. But what did you *gain* by this?

HOLMES

Her confidence, and so far as I was able to secure it, her regard. As I cannot obtain possession of the letters, photographs, and jewelry in that packet without her consent, my only alternative is to obtain that consent—to induce her to give it to me of her own free will. Its return to her after I had laid hands on it was the first step in this direction. The second will depend entirely upon what transpires today. I expect Forman here to report in half an hour.

(*Light hurried footsteps outside R. Short quick knock at door and enter* TÉRÈSE *at door up R. in great haste and excitement.* WATSON *rises and turns and faces her near table.* HOLMES *turns toward fireplace*)

TÉRÈSE

(*Up R.C.*)

I beg you to pardon me, mesure, ze boy he say to come right up as soon as I come.

HOLMES

Quite right! Quite right.

TÉRÈSE

(*Moves down R.C. a little*)

Ah. I fear me zere is trouble—messieurs—ze butlair—your assestant—ze one who sent me to you—

HOLMES

Forman?

(*Turning to her*)

TÉRÈSE

Ah, heem! Forman! Zere eez somesing done to heem! I fear to go down to see.

HOLMES

Down where?

(*Coming to C. above table.*

WATSON *goes over to near fire L. and watches scene*)

TÉRÈSE

Ze down.

(*Gesture*)

Ze cellaire of zat house. Eet ees a dreadful place. He deed not come back. He went down—he deed not come up.

(*Business of anguish.*

HOLMES *goes to table—rings bell and takes revolver from drawer and slides it into his hip pocket, at same time unfastening dressing gown*)

HOLMES

(*During business*)

Who sent him down?

TÉRÈSE

M'sieur of ze house, M'sieur Chetwood.

HOLMES

Larrabee.

TÉRÈSE

Oui.

HOLMES

(*During business*)

Has he been down there long?

TÉRÈSE

No—for I soon suspect—ze dreadful noise was heard. Oh—
 (*Covers face*)
—ze noise! Ze noise!

HOLMES

What noise?
 (*Goes to her and seizes her arm*)

TÉRÈSE

Ze noise!

HOLMES

Try to be calm and answer me. What did it sound like?

TÉRÈSE

Ze dreadful cry of a man who eez struck down by some deadly
seeng.
 (*Enter* BILLY *up R.*)

HOLMES

(*Moving quickly to R.C.*)

Coat—boots, and order a cab—quick.
 (*Back again to table, takes a second revolver out*)

BILLY

(*Darting off at door up L.*)

Yes, sir.

HOLMES

(*To* TÉRÈSE)

Did anyone follow him down?

(BILLY *is back in a second*)

TÉRÈSE

I did not see.

HOLMES

Don't wait. Order the cab.

(BILLY *shoots off at door up R., having placed coat over Chesterfield and boots on floor*)

The game's afoot, Watson. Take this, come with me.

(*Handing* WATSON *a revolver.* WATSON *advances a step to meet* HOLMES *and takes revolver*)

TÉRÈSE

I had not better go also?

HOLMES

No . . . Wait here!

(*Ready to go. About to take off dressing gown near L.C.*

Hurried footsteps heard outside up R.

Pause)

Ha! But I hear Forman now.

(*Enter* FORMAN *up R.*)

TÉRÈSE

(*Seeing* FORMAN—*under her breath*)

Ah!

(Backing a little to R.

FORMAN *coming rapidly on, is covered with black coal stains, and his clothing otherwise stained. He has a bad bruise on his forehead. But he must not be made to look grotesque. There must be no suspicion of comedy about his entrance. Also, he must not be torn, as* BILLY *is later in the scene.* HOLMES *just above table, stops taking off his dressing gown, slips it back on his shoulders again)*

FORMAN

(To HOLMES, *coming C. in an entirely matter-of-fact tone)*

Nothing more last night, sir. After you left, Prince came in, and they made a start for her room to get the package away, but I gave the three knocks with an ax on the floor beams as you directed, and they didn't get any farther. But then this morning, a little after nine—

HOLMES

One moment.

FORMAN

Yes, sir?

(Takes step up C.)

HOLMES

(Quietly turns to TÉRÈSE)

Mademoiselle—step into that room and rest yourself.

(Indicating door down R.)

TÉRÈSE

(Who has been standing down R. deeply interested in FORMAN'S *report, shaking head)*

But I am not tired, monsieur.

HOLMES

Then step into that room and walk about a bit. I'll let you know when you are required.

TERESE

(*After an instant's pause, sees it*)

Oui, monsieur.

(*Exit at door down R.*

HOLMES *goes over and quietly closes the door after her—he then turns to* WATSON, *but remains at the door with right ear alert to catch any sound from within*)

HOLMES

Take a look at his head, Watson.

(*Listens at door.*

WATSON *at once goes to* FORMAN *up C.*)

FORMAN

It's nothing at all.

HOLMES

Take a look at his head, Watson.

WATSON

An ugly bruise, but . . . um . . . not dangerous.

(*Examining head.*

WATSON *goes quickly L. a little, and stands near end of Chesterfield, facing around to* FORMAN)

HOLMES

Very well . . . At a little after nine, you say—

(HOLMES *has attention on door at R., where* TÉRÈSE *went off, while listening to* FORMAN—*but not in such a*

90   SHERLOCK HOLMES

*marked way as to take the attention off from what he
says, and after a few seconds sits on Chesterfield R.)*

FORMAN

Yes, sir.

(Coming down R.C. a little)

FORMAN *(Continued)*

A little after nine, Larrabee and his wife drove away and she
came back about eleven without him. A little later, old Leuftner
came and the two went to work in the library. I got a look at
them from the outside and found they were making up a *counterfeit of the package we are working for!* You'll have to watch
for some sharp trick, sir.

HOLMES

No, *they'll* have to watch for the sharp trick, Forman! And Larrabee, what of him?

FORMAN

He came back a little after three.

HOLMES

How did he seem?

FORMAN

Under great excitement, sir.

HOLMES

Any marked resentment toward you?

FORMAN

I think there was, sir—though he tried not to show it.

HOLMES

He has consulted someone outside. Was the Larrabee woman's
behavior different also?

FORMAN

She gave me an ugly look as she came in.

HOLMES

Ah, an ugly look. She was present at the consultation. They were advised to get rid of you. He sent you down into the cellar on some pretext. You were attacked in the dark by two men—possibly three—men—you received a bad blow from a sand club. You succeeded in striking down one of your assailants with a stone. No! a piece of timber and escaped from the others in the dark, crawling out through a coal grating.

FORMAN

That's what took place, sir.

HOLMES

They have taken in a partner, and a dangerous one at that. He not only directed this conspiracy against you, but he also advised the making of the counterfeit package. Within a very short time I shall hear from Mr. Larrabee offering to sell me this package. He will indicate that Miss Faulkner has changed her mind and has concluded to get what she can for them. He will desire to meet me on the subject—he will then endeavor to sell me his bogus package for an enormous sum of money. After that—

(*Enter* BILLY *door up R. with a letter—comes down R. to* HOLMES)

BILLY

Letter, sir! Most important letter, sir!

(*After giving* HOLMES *letter, he stands waiting*)

HOLMES

Unless I am greatly mistaken—the said communication is at hand.

(*Lightly waves letters across before face once as if getting the scent*)

It is. Read it for me, Watson, there's a good fellow—my eyes—

> (*With a motion across eyes, half smile*)

cocaine, you know—all those things you like so much.

> (BILLY *goes with letter to* WATSON. WATSON *takes letter and goes up to lamp*)

WATSON

> (*Opens letter and reads*)

"Dear sir."

> (*After* WATSON *is at lamp,* FORMAN *goes upstage and waits C.*)

HOLMES

Who—thus—addresses me?

> (*Slides further onto Chesterfield, supporting head on pillows*)

WATSON

> (*Glances at signature*)

"James Larrabee."

HOLMES

> (*Whimsically*)

What a surprise! And what has James to say this evening?

WATSON

"Dear sir."

HOLMES

I do hope he won't say that again.

WATSON

"I have the honor to inform you that Miss Faulkner has changed her mind regarding the letters, etc., which you wish to obtain and has decided to dispose of them for a monetary consideration. She has placed them in my hands for this purpose, and if you are in a position to offer a good round sum, and to pay it down at once in cash, the entire lot is yours. If you wish to negotiate, however, it must be tonight, at the house of a friend of mine, in the city. At eleven o'clock you will be at the Guards' Monument at the foot of Waterloo Place. You will see a cab with wooden shutters to the windows. Enter it and the driver will bring you to my friend's house. If you have the cab followed, or try any other underhand trick, you won't get what you want. Let me know your decision. Yours truly, James Larrabee."

(HOLMES, *during the reading of the letter, begins to write something in a perfectly leisurely way. The light of the fire is upon him, shining across the room—on his left—as he writes*)

HOLMES

Now see if I have the points. Tonight, eleven o'clock, Guards' Monument, Waterloo Place, cab with wooden shutters. No one to accompany me. No one to follow cab—or I don't get what I want.

WATSON

Quite right.

HOLMES

Ah!

WATSON

But this cab with the wooden shutters.

HOLMES

A simple device to keep me from seeing where I am driven. Billy!

BILLY

(*Going to* HOLMES *at once*)

Yes, sir.

HOLMES

(*Reaching out letter to* BILLY *back of him without looking*)

Who brought it?

BILLY

It was a woman, sir.

HOLMES

(*Slight dead stop as he is handing letter*)

Ah—old or young?

(*He does not look around for these questions, but faces as he was, front or nearly so*)

BILLY

Werry old, sir.

HOLMES

In a cab?

BILLY

Yes, sir.

HOLMES

Seen the driver before?

BILLY

Yes, sir—but I can't think where.

HOLMES

(*Rising*)

Very well. Hand this to the old lady—apologize for the delay, and take a good look at that driver again.

(*Moves R.*)

BILLY

(*Takes letter*)

Yes, sir.

(*Exits at door up R.*)

WATSON

But surely, Holmes—you didn't say that you would go?

(*Coming down R.C.*)

HOLMES

Certainly I did.

WATSON

But it's the counterfeit.

HOLMES

(*Moves toward door R.*)

The counterfeit is exactly what I want.

WATSON

(*C.*)

Oh! But why so?

HOLMES

(*Turning to* WATSON *an instant at R.*)

Because with it I shall obtain the original.

HOLMES (*Continued*)

(*Turns and speaks off at door R.*)

Mademoiselle!

(*Turns back and moves R.C.*)

WATSON

Yes . . . But this fellow means mischief.

(*Enter* TÉRÈSE. *She comes into and stands a little way inside the room*)

HOLMES

(*R.C. facing* WATSON—*touching himself lightly*)

This fellow means the same.

(*As* HOLMES *turns away to* TÉRÈSE, WATSON *crosses L. and stands with back to fire.*

To TÉRÈSE)

Mademoiselle, be so good as to listen to every word. Tonight at twelve o'clock I meet Mr. James Larrabee and purchase from him the false bundle of letters to which you just now heard us refer, as you were listening at the keyhole of that door.

TÉRÈSE

(*Slightly confused, but staring blankly*)

Oui, monsieur.

HOLMES

I wish Miss Faulkner to know at once that I propose to buy this package tonight.

TÉRÈSE

I will tell her, monsieur.

HOLMES

That is my wish. But do not tell her that I know this packet and its contents to be counterfeit. She is to suppose that I think I am buying the genuine.

TÉRÈSE

Oh, *oui, monsieur, je comprends*. When you purchase you think you have the *real*.

HOLMES

Precisely.

(*Motions her up to door up R. and moving toward door with her*)

One thing more. I shall ask you tomorrow evening to accompany her to this place where Sir Edward Leighton and Count Von Stalburg will be to receive the package at my hands. But you will receive further instructions as to this in the morning.

TÉRÈSE

Oui, monsieur.

> (*Turns and exits at once at door up R.*)

HOLMES

(*Up R.*)

Forman. Put on your beggar disguise Number 14 and go through every den in Limehouse and Wapping. Don't stop till you get a clue to this new partner of the Larrabees. I must have that.

> (*Turns away to L. toward* WATSON)

I must have that.

FORMAN

Very good, sir.

> (*Just about to go.*
>
> Enter BILLY *at door up R. just within and down R. a little*)

BILLY

If you please, sir, there's a man a-waitin' at the street door—and 'e says 'e must speak to Mr. Forman, sir, as quick as 'e can.

> (HOLMES—*who was moving toward L.—stops suddenly and stands motionless—eyes front above table C. Pause.*
>
> *Music. Danger. Melodramatic. Very low. Agitato. B string*)

HOLMES

(*After a pause*)

I think we'd better have a look at that man. Billy, show him up.

BILLY

'E can't come up, sir—'e's a-watchin' a man in the street. 'E says 'e's from Scotland Yard.

FORMAN

(*Going toward door*)

I'd better see what it is, sir.

HOLMES

No!

(FORMAN *stops. Pause. Music heard throughout this pause, but without swelling forte in the least.* HOLMES *stands motionless a moment*)

HOLMES (*Continued*)

Very well—

(*A motion indicating* FORMAN *to go*)

But—take a look at him first. Be ready for anything.

FORMAN

Trust me for that, sir.

(*Exit at door up R.*)

HOLMES

(*C.*)

See what he does, Billy.

BILLY

Yes, sir.

(HOLMES *stands an instant thinking*)

WATSON

This is becoming interesting.

> (HOLMES *does not reply. He goes up to near door up
> R. and listens, then moves to window and glances
> down to street, then turns and goes down to table*)

Now look here, Holmes, you've given me a halfway look into this
case—

HOLMES

> (*Looking up at him*)

What case?

WATSON

This strange case of—Miss—

HOLMES

Quite so. One moment, my dear fellow.

> (*Rings bell*)

Ring the bell, Watson.

> (*After slight wait, enter* BILLY *at door up R.*)

Mr. Forman—he is still there?

BILLY

> (*At door up R.*)

No, sir—'e's gone.

> (*Second's pause*)

HOLMES

That's all.

BILLY

Yes, sir. Thank you, sir.

> (*Exit at door up R.
> Music stops*)

HOLMES

As you were saying, my dear Doctor,

 (*Eyes front*)

This strange case—of—

 (*Stops, but does not change position. As if listening or thinking*)

WATSON

Of . . . um . . . Miss Faulkner.

HOLMES

 (*Abandoning further anxiety and giving attention to* WATSON)

Precisely. This strange case of Miss Faulkner.

 (*Eyes down an instant as he recalls it*)

WATSON

Now look here, Holmes,

 (*Coming to L. of table*)

You've given me some idea of it. Don't you think it would be only fair to let me have the rest?

 (HOLMES *looks at him*)

HOLMES

What shall I tell you?

 (*Above table a little to R.*)

WATSON

You could tell me what you propose to do with that counterfeit package—which you are going *to risk your life to obtain.*

 (HOLMES *looks at* WATSON *an instant before speaking*)

HOLMES

Oh, my life is worth nothing when I defend so heroic a purpose. I shall assist a man who robbed a young girl of life and honor to rob her sister of her property. I shall accomplish this by a piece of trickery and deceit of which I am heartily ashamed—and which I would never have undertaken—if I had known more—as I do now—

(*Looks to the front absently*)

It's too bad, Watson. She's rather a nice girl.

(*Goes over to mantel and gets a pipe.*

As HOLMES *crosses,* WATSON *comes R. of table, passing behind it*)

WATSON

(*Following* HOLMES *with his eyes*)

Nice girl, eh?

(HOLMES *nods "Yes" to* WATSON. *Brief pause. He turns with pipe in hands and glances toward* WATSON, *then down*)

Then you think that possibly—

(*Enter* BILLY *quickly, at door up R.*)

BILLY

I beg pardon, sir, Mr. Forman's just sent out from the chemist's on the corner to say 'is 'ead is a-hurt' 'im a bit, an' would Dr. Watson—

(WATSON *on hearing his name, turns and looks in direction of* BILLY)

—kindly step over and get 'im something to put on it.

WATSON

(*Moving at once toward door up R.*)

Yes—certainly—I'll go at once.

(*Picking up hat off chair R.*)

That's singular.

(*Stands puzzled R.C.*)

It didn't look like anything serious.

(*At door up R.*)

Never mind, Holmes, I'll be back in a minute.

(*Exits.*

HOLMES, *standing L., says nothing*)

HOLMES

Billy. Who brought that message from Forman?

BILLY

Boy from the chemist's, sir.

HOLMES

Yes, of course, but which boy?

BILLY

I couldn't see clearly, he stood a few yards off in the fog, but I'm sure I ain't seen him before—he was pretty big for a chemist's boy.

HOLMES

Now, quick, Billy, run down and look after the doctor. If the boy's gone and there's a man with him it means mischief. Let me know quickly. Don't stop to come up, ring the door bell. I'll hear it. Ring it loud. Quick now.

BILLY

Yes, sir.

(*Exit quickly at door up R.*

HOLMES *waits motionless at L. a moment, listening.*

Music heard very faintly.

HOLMES *moves quickly toward door up R. When half-way to the door, he stops suddenly, listening; then be-gins to glide backward toward table down C., stops and listens—eyes to the front; turns toward door up*

R. listening. Pipe in left hand—waits—sees pipe in hand—picks up match—lights pipe, listening, and suddenly shouts of warning from BILLY—*turns—at the same time picking up revolver from off table and puts in pocket of dressing gown, with his hand still clasping it.* HOLMES *at once assumes easy attitude, but keeping eyes on door. Enter* MORIARTY *at door up R. He walks in at door very quietly and deliberately. Stops just within doorway, and looks fixedly at* HOLMES, *then moves forward a little way. His right hand is behind his back. As* MORIARTY *moves forward,* HOLMES *makes slight motion for the purpose of keeping him covered with a revolver in his pocket.* MORIARTY, *seeing what* HOLMES *is doing, stops*)

BILLY

Sir! Sir!

MORIARTY

Now that's a dangerous habit to finger loaded firearms in the pocket of one's dressing gown.

HOLMES

You'll go straight from here to the hospital if you keep that hand behind you.

MORIARTY

You obviously don't know me.

HOLMES

On the contrary, I think it is fairly evident that I do. I could give you five minutes if you've got anything to say.

(MORIARTY *moves his right hand as if to take something from inside his coat*)

What are you about to do?

MORIARTY

Look at my watch.

HOLMES

I'll tell you when the five minutes are up. Pray take a chair.

MORIARTY

All that I have to say has already crossed your mind.

HOLMES

Then my answer has already crossed yours.

MORIARTY

You stand fast?

HOLMES

Absolutely.

> (MORIARTY *puts his hand to his pocket.* HOLMES *raises his six-shooter, and* MORIARTY *produces a memorandum pad*)

MORIARTY

You crossed my path on the fourth of September. On the twenty-third you incommoded me; by the middle of October I was seriously inconvenienced by you; at the end of October I was absolutely hampered in my plans; and now at the close of November I find myself placed in such a position through your continual persecution that I am in positive danger of losing my liberty. The situation is becoming an impossible one.

HOLMES

Have you any suggestion to make?

MORIARTY

You must drop it, Mr. Holmes, you really must, you know.

HOLMES

After Monday.

MORIARTY

I am quite sure that a man of your intelligence will see that there can be but one outcome to this affair. It is necessary that you should withdraw. You have managed things in such a way that we have only one recourse left. It has been an intellectual treat to me to see the way you have grappled with this affair, and I say unaffectedly, it would be a grief to me to be forced to take any extreme measure. You smile, sir, but I assure you that it really would, you know.

HOLMES

Danger is part of my trade.

MORIARTY

This is not danger, this is inevitable destruction. You stand in the way not merely of an individual but of a mighty organization, the full extent of which you, with all your cleverness, have been unable to realize.

(MORIARTY *again stopped with his hands at breast pocket*)

HOLMES

Get your hands down.

(MORIARTY *does not lower his hands at first request*)

MORIARTY

(*Lowers hands to his lap. Slight pause, raising hands again slowly as he speaks*)

Why, I was merely about to . . .

HOLMES

Merely don't do it.

(*Remonstratingly—his hands still up near his breast*)

If you want to replace that memorandum book so badly I'll have someone replace it for you.

(MORIARTY *slowly lowers his hands again.*

Rings a bell on table with left hand)

I like to save my guests unnecessary trouble.

(*Short wait*)

MORIARTY

(*After pause*)

Ah, doesn't it occur to you, Mr. Holmes, he may possibly have been detained?

HOLMES

It does. But I also observe *you to be in very much the same predicament.*

(*Pause.*

HOLMES *rings the bell for the second time. Noise on stairway outside R. Enter* BILLY *up R. with part of his coat, and with sleeves of shirt and waistcoat badly torn.*

Music stops)

BILLY

(*Up near door*)

I beg pardon, sir—someone tried to 'old me, sir!

(*Panting for breath*)

HOLMES

It's evident, however, that he failed to do so.

BILLY

Yes, sir—'e's got my coat, sir, but 'e 'asn't got *me!*

HOLMES

Billy!

BILLY

Yes, sir?

> (BILLY *moves down C., back of table—still out of breath*)

HOLMES

The gentleman that I am pointing out to you with this revolver wishes to replace a memorandum book which he took some time ago from his right hand inside coat pocket. He now wishes to return it, however, into his left hand inside coat pocket.

> (MORIARTY *gives a very slight start or movement of right hand to breast pocket, getting it almost to his pocket, then recollecting himself, seeing that Holmes has got him covered*)

As he is quite clearly not himself today and the exertion might prove injurious, suppose you attend to it.

BILLY

Yes, sir.

> (*He goes quickly to* MORIARTY, *puts hand in his pocket and draws out a bulldog revolver*)

HOLMES

No.

BILLY

Look at this, sir.

HOLMES

Quite so. Put it on the table.

> (MORIARTY *makes a grab for it.*
>
> BILLY *places it so that it is within easy reach of* HOLMES)

BILLY

Shall I see if he's got another, sir?

HOLMES

Why, Billy, you do disappoint me; the gentleman has taken the trouble to inform you that he hasn't got another one.

BILLY

When, sir?

HOLMES

When he made that snatch for this one. Well now, Professor, do you think of anything else you'd like?

(MORIARTY *does not reply*)

Any other little thing you've got, that you want while Billy's here? No, I'm sorry, that's all, Billy.

(*Pause.* MORIARTY, *motionless, eyes on* HOLMES. HOLMES *puts his own revolver in his pocket quietly.* MORIARTY *remains motionless, his eyes on* HOLMES, *waiting for a chance*)

BILLY

Thank you, sir.

(*Exit at door up R.*

HOLMES *carelessly picks up* MORIARTY'S *weapon, turns it over in his hands a little below table for a moment, then tosses it back on table again—during which business* MORIARTY *looks front savagely*)

HOLMES

(*Tapping revolver with pipe*)

Rather a rash project of yours, Moriarty—even if you have made the street secure in every respect—to think of using that thing—so early in the evening and in this part of town. I am afraid that in the pleasure of this conversation I am neglecting business which requires my presence elsewhere.

MORIARTY

Ah yes, well, well. It seems a pity, but I have done what I could. I know every move of your game. You hope to place me in the dock. I tell you that I will never stand in the dock. You hope to beat me. I tell you that you will never beat me. And if you are clever enough to bring destruction upon me, rest assured I will do as much to you.

HOLMES

You have paid me several compliments, Moriarty, let me pay you one in return when I say that could I be assured of your destruction I would cheerfully in the interests of the public, accept my own.

MORIARTY

(*Nearing* HOLMES *and looking toward door R.*)

I came here this evening to see if *peace* could not be arranged between us.

HOLMES

Ah yes.

(*Smiling pleasantly and pressing tobacco in pipe*)

I saw that. That's rather good.

MORIARTY

(*Passionately*)

You have seen fit not only to reject my proposals, but to make insulting references coupled with threats of arrest.

HOLMES

Quite so! Quite so!

(*Lights match and holds it to pipe*)

MORIARTY

(*Moving a little so as to be nearer table*)

Well—

(Slyly picking up revolver)

—you do not heed my warning—perhaps you will heed this!

(Making a sudden plunge and aiming at HOLMES's *head, he rapidly snaps the revolver in quick attempt to fire.*

HOLMES *turns quietly toward him, still holding match to pipe so that the last snap of hammer is directly in his face. Very slight pause on* MORIARTY's *being unable to fire—and backing up C., at same time boiling with rage.*

HOLMES, *as if recollecting something, tosses away match, and feeling quickly in left pocket of dressing gown, brings out some cartridges and tosses them carelessly on table toward* MORIARTY.

Enter BILLY)

HOLMES

Billy!

BILLY

Yes, sir!

HOLMES

Show this gentleman nicely to the door.

BILLY

Yes, sir! This way, sir!

(Standing within door up R.)

MORIARTY

Touché, M'Holmes. Auf Wiedersehen.

*(*PROFESSOR MORIARTY *looks at* HOLMES *a moment, then flings revolver down and across the table, clenches fist in* HOLMES's *face, turns, boiling with rage, picks hat up, and exits quickly at door up R., muttering aloud as he goes)*

HOLMES

(*After exit of* MORIARTY)

Billy!

BILLY

Yes, sir!

(BILLY *comes quickly down*)

HOLMES

You're a good boy.

BILLY

Yes, sir! Thank you, sir!

(*Stands grinning up at* HOLMES)

HOLMES

Now get me a cab to go to Waterloo Place.

(*The LIGHTS GO OUT suddenly*)

CURTAIN

ACT II

Scene 1

The gas chamber at Stepney. A large, dark, grimy room on an upper floor of an old building backing on wharves, etc. Plaster cracking off masonry piers or chimney showing. As uncanny and gruesome appearance as possible. Heavy beams and timbers showing. Door down L. leads to the landing and then to the entrance. The door up L.C. leads to a small cupboard. The walls of the cupboard can be seen when the door is opened. Large window up R.C., closed. Grimy and dirty glass so nothing can be seen through it. The window is nailed with spike nails securely shut. Black backing—no light behind. Strong bars outside back of windows, to show when window is broken. These bars must not be seen through the glass. Trash all over the room. The only light in the room on the rise of the curtain is from a dim lantern—carried on by MC TAGUE.

Characteristic Music for Curtain.

CRAIGIN *and* LEARY *are discovered.* CRAIGIN *is sitting on a box R. He sits glum and motionless, waiting.* LEARY *is sitting on table, his feet on the chair in front of it.*

Door L. opens and MC TAGUE *enters with safety lamp. He stops just within a moment, glancing around in the dimness. Soon moves up near a masonry pier on the L., a little above the door, and leans against it waiting.* CRAIGIN, LEARY, *and* MC TAGUE *are dressed in dark clothes and wear felt-soled shoes.*

McTAGUE

Here we are then.

LEARY

What's Mc Tague doing 'ere?

McTAGUE

I was sent 'ere.

LEARY

I thought the Seraph was gonna be with us on this job.

CRAIGIN

'E ain't.

LEARY

Who was the last person you put the gas on in this place.

(*Pause*)

CRAIGIN

I didn't 'ear 'is name.

(*Pause*)

'E'd been 'oldin' back money on a job out some railway place.

(*Pause*)

McTAGUE

What's this 'ere job 'e wants done?

(*Sits on box L., placing lamp on floor by his side. Pause*)

CRAIGIN

I ain't been told.

(Pause)

LEARY

As long as it's 'ere we know what it's likely to be. Pssss!

(Door opens slowly and hesitatingly. Enter SID PRINCE *L. He stands just within door, and looks about a little suspiciously as if uncertain what to do. Pause. He notices that the door is slowly closing behind him and quietly holds it back. But he must not burlesque this movement with funny business.* MC TAGUE *holds lantern up to see who it is, at the same time rising and coming down near* PRINCE*)*

PRINCE

Does any one of you blokes know if this is the place where I meet Alf Bassick?

(Pause. Neither of the other men take notice of PRINCE. MC TAGUE *goes back to where he was sitting before* PRINCE'S *entrance)*

PRINCE *(Continued)*

(After waiting a moment)

From wot you say, I take it you don't.

CRAIGIN

We ain't knowin' no such man. 'E may be 'ere and 'e may not.

PRINCE

Oh!

(Comes a little farther into room, to L.C., and lets the door close)

That's quite all right then, thanks very much.

(Pause. No one speaks)

Nice old place to find, this 'ere is.

(*No one answers him*)

And when you do find it—

(*Looks about*)

—I can't say it's any too cheerful.

(*Coming C. He thereupon pulls out a cigarette case, puts a cigarette in his mouth and feels in pocket for matches. Finds one. About to light it. Has moved a few steps during this*)

CRAIGIN

Here!

(PRINCE *stops*)

Don't light that! . . . It ain't safe!

(PRINCE *stops motionless, where above speech caught him, for an instant. Pause.* PRINCE *begins to turn his head slowly and only a little way, glances carefully about, as if expecting to see tins of nitroglycerine. He sees nothing on either side, and finally turns toward* CRAIGIN)

PRINCE

If it ain't seekin' too much, wot's the matter with the place? It looks all right to me.

CRAIGIN

Well, don't light no matches, and it'll stay lookin' the same.

(*Pause. Door opens, and* BASSICK *enters hurriedly at L. He looks quickly about*)

BASSICK

(*Near L.C.*)

Oh, there you are, Prince. I was looking for you outside.

PRINCE

(*Going L. to* BASSICK)

You told me to be 'ere, sir. That was 'ow the last arrangement
stood.

BASSICK

Very well!

(*Going across* PRINCE *to C. and glancing about to see
that the other men are present*)

Have you got the rope, Craigin?

(*Voices are still kept low*)

CRAIGIN

(*Pointing to bunch of loose rope on floor near him*)

It's 'ere.

(PRINCE *remains L.C., listening and turning to men as
they are spoken to*)

BASSICK

That you, Leary?

LEARY

(*Up C.*)

'Ere, sir!

(PRINCE *looks up toward* LEARY)

BASSICK

And McTague?

McTAGUE

(*At L.*)

'Ere, sir!

(PRINCE *turns toward* McTAGUE, *backing a little toward door L.*)

BASSICK

You want to be very careful with it tonight—you've got a tough one.

CRAIGIN

You ain't said who, as I've 'eard.

BASSICK

Sherlock Holmes.

CRAIGIN

(*After the pause*)

You mean that, sir?

BASSICK

Indeed I do!

CRAIGIN

We're goin' to count *'im* out.

BASSICK

Well, if you *don't* and he gets away—well, I'm sorry for you, that's all.

CRAIGIN

I'll be a bit pleased to turn the gas on 'im—I tell you *that*.

LEARY

Interfering stuck-up nob!

(*Sound of* MORIARTY *and* LARRABEE *coming*)

BASSICK

Sh! Professor Moriarty's coming.

(MC TAGUE *places lamp on box at R.*)

LEARY

Not the guv'nor?

BASSICK

Yes. He wanted to see to this.

(*The three men retire R. a little upstage, waiting.*
BASSICK *moves toward C. to meet* MORIARTY. PRINCE
moves up out of way on L. Door L. opens. Enter
MORIARTY *followed by* LARRABEE. *Door slowly closes
behind him.* LARRABEE *waits a moment near door L.
and then retires up near* PRINCE. *They watch the following scene from up L.C. All speeches low—quiet—
in undertone*)

MORIARTY

(*L.C.*)

Where's Craigin?

CRAIGIN

'Ere, sir.

(CRAIGIN *steps forward on R. side*)

MORIARTY

(*Crosses to R.C.*)

Have you got your men?

CRAIGIN

All 'ere, sir.

MORIARTY

No *mistakes* tonight, Craigin.

CRAIGIN

Right, sir.

MORIARTY

(*Quick glance about*)

Bassick, that door.

(*Points up L.C. back to audience*)

BASSICK

A small cupboard, sir.

(*Goes quickly up and opens the door wide to show it.* LEARY *catches up lantern at R. and swings it near the cupboard door*)

MORIARTY

(*Moving up C.*)

No outlet?

BASSICK

(*L. of cupboard*)

None whatever, sir.

(LEARY *swings lantern almost inside cupboard to let* MORIARTY *see. All this dialogue in very low tones, but distinct and impressive.* BASSICK *closes door after lantern business*)

MORIARTY

(*Turns and points up C.*)

That window?

BASSICK

(*Moving over a little toward up C.*)

Nailed down, sir!

(LEARY *turns to R. and swings the lantern near window so that* MORIARTY *can see*)

MORIARTY

(*Up C.*)

A man might break the glass.

BASSICK

If he did that he'd come against heavy iron bars outside.

CRAIGIN

We'll 'ave 'im tied down afore 'e could break any glass, sir.

MORIARTY

(*Who has turned to* CRAIGIN)

Ah! You've used it before. Of course, is it airtight?

BASSICK

Every crevice is caulked, sir.

MORIARITY

And the gas?

(*Satisfaction. Glances at door L., through which he entered*)

When the men turn the gas on him they leave through that door?

BASSICK

Yes, sir.

MORIARTY

It can be made quite secure?

BASSICK

It's heavily bolted, sir.

MORIARTY

Let me see how quickly you can operate them.

BASSICK

They tie the man down, sir—there's no need to hurry.

MORIARTY

(*Same voice*)

Let me see how quickly you can operate them.

BASSICK

(*Quick voice*)

Leary!

(Motions him to door L., at same time giving two or three steps up and to L.C.)

LEARY

(Handing lamp to CRAIGIN)

Yes, sir!

(He jumps to door L., and goes out, closing it at once, and immediately the sounds of sliding bolts and the dropping of bars is heard from outside L.

This is a very important effect, as it is repeated at the end of the Act. CRAIGIN places lamp on box at R.

Sounds of bolts withdrawn and LEARY enters at door L. and waits)

MORIARTY

(Goes R. to CRAIGIN)

Craigin—you take your men outside that door and wait until Mr. Larrabee has had a little business interview with the gentlemen. Take them up the passage to the left so that Holmes does not see them as he comes in.

(To BASSICK)

Who's driving the cab tonight?

(Speaks from position at R.)

BASSICK

I sent O'Hagan. His orders are to drive him about for an hour so he doesn't know the distance or the direction he's going, and then stop at the small door at Upper Swandem Lane. He's going to get him out there and show him up to this door.

MORIARTY

The cab windows were covered, of course?

BASSICK

Wooden shutters, sir, bolted and secure. There isn't a place he can see through the size of a pin. And there's the fog.

MORIARTY

(Satisfied)

Ah! . . .

(Looks about—going to C. and half up)

We need a lamp here.

BASSICK

Better not, sir—there might be some gas left.

MORIARTY

(Well up C.)

Why, you've got a lamp there.

(Pointing to miner's safety lamp on box at R.)

BASSICK

It's a safety lamp, sir.

MORIARTY

Oh, that's a safety lamp, sir! The minute he sees that he will know what we are up to and we're finished. We're finished.

(Sniffs)

There's no gas. Here! Go and tell Lascar we need a good lamp.

(BASSICK exits L.

Looks about up R.C.)

Bring that table over here.

(Pointing down R.C.

CRAIGIN *and* MC TAGUE *bring table from upstage and place it down R.C.* MC TAGUE *R. of table as they bring it down.* CRAIGIN *L.)*

Now, Craigin—and the rest of you— One thing—remember. No shooting tonight! Not a single shot. It can be heard in the alley below. The first thing is to get his revolver away from him. Two of you attract his attention in front—one of you come up from behind and snatch it out of his pocket. Then you have him. Is that clear, Craigin?

CRAIGIN

I'll attend to it, sir.

> (*The three men retire to R. Enter* BASSICK *at door L. with large lamp. Glass shade to lamp of whitish color.*
>
> BASSICK *crosses to table and places lamp near L. end of table, standing at lower side of table with back to front. Lights on stronger from foots and border when the lamp is brought in*)

BASSICK

> (*To* MC TAGUE)

Put out that lamp.

> (MC TAGUE *is about to pick up lamp*)

CRAIGIN

Stop!

> (MC TAGUE *waits*)

We'll want this when the other's taken away.

BASSICK

He mustn't see it, understand.

MORIARTY

> (*Up C.*)

Don't put it out—cover it with something.

CRAIGIN

Here! Them boxes.

(He goes up to R., takes lantern and pulling out a large box from several others R., places lantern within and pushes the open side against the wall so that no light from lantern can be seen from front.

LEARY *moves over to R., following* CRAIGIN *up R., as if to assist in the business)*

BASSICK

(Approaching MORIARTY *C.)*

You should be going, sir. O'Hagan might be a little early. That will do.

(Crosses to door down L. and stands waiting)

MORIARTY

(C.)

Mr. Larrabee—you understand! They are waiting for you. I give you this opportunity to get what you can for your trouble. But anything that is found on him after you have finished—is subject—

(Glances at CRAIGIN *and others)*

—to the usual division.

LARRABEE

That's all I want.

MORIARTY

When you have quite finished and got your money, suppose you blow that little whistle which I observe hanging from your watch chain—and these gentlemen will take *their* turn.

*(*BASSICK *at door L., holds door open for* MORIARTY.

LARRABEE *moves up out of way as* MORIARTY *crosses to door L. At door, turning to* CRAIGIN*)*

And, Craigin—

CRAIGIN

Sir?

(CRAIGIN *crosses to* MORIARTY *at L.*)

MORIARTY

At the proper moment present my compliments to Mr. Sherlock Holmes and say, I wish him a pleasant journey to the other side.

(*Exits at door L., followed by* BASSICK.

LEARY *and* MCTAGUE *remain up R. and R.C. a moment after* MORIARTY'S *exit and* CRAIGIN *joins them.* LARRABEE *near table C., glances about critically. As* MORIARTY *exits,* PRINCE *throws cigarette on floor in disgust, which* LEARY *picks up as he exits later, putting it in his pocket*)

LARRABEE

You'd better put that rope out of sight.

CRAIGIN

(*Joins* LEARY *and* MCTAGUE *at door L. Speaks to* LARRABEE *from door*)

You understand, sir, we'll be around the far turn of the passage —so 'e won't see us as 'e's comin' up.

LARRABEE

I understand.

(*Turning to* CRAIGIN)

CRAIGIN

An' it's w'en we 'ears that whistle, eh?

LARRABEE

When you hear that whistle.

(*By lamp R.C.*)

PRINCE

(*Coming down in a grumpy manner, head down, not looking at* LARRABEE)

Look 'ere, Jim, this sort of thing ain't exactly my line.

LARRABEE

(*At table R.C.*)

I suppose not.

PRINCE

(*Still eyes about without looking at* LARRABEE)

When it comes to blowing a safe or drillin' into bank vaults, I feel perfectly at 'ome, but I don't care so much to see a man—

(*Stops—hesitates*)

Well, it ain't my line!

LARRABEE

(*Turning*)

Here!

(*Going to him and urging him toward door L. and putting package away*)

All I want you to do is go out to the corner of the street and let me know when he comes.

PRINCE

(*Stops and turns to* LARRABEE)

'Ow will I let you know?

LARRABEE

Have you got a cab whistle?

PRINCE

(*Pulls one out of pocket*)

Cert'nly.

LARRABEE

Well, when you see O'Hagan driving with him, come down the alley there and blow it twice.

(*Urging* PRINCE *a little nearer door L.*)

PRINCE

Yes—but ain't that quite likely to call a cab at the same time?

LARRABEE

What more do you want—take the cab and go home.

PRINCE

Oh, you won't need me 'ere again. Then?

LARRABEE

No.

(PRINCE *turns to go at door L.*)

PRINCE

(*Going to door—very much relieved*)

Oh, very well—then I'll tear myself away.

(*Exit at door L.*)

LARRABEE

How did you get to this place?

ALICE

I followed you—in a cab.

LARRABEE

What have you been doing since I came up here? Informing the police, perhaps.

ALICE

I was afraid he'd come—so I waited.

LARRABEE

Oh—to warn him very likely?

ALICE

Yes.
(Pause)
To warn him.
(Looks about room)

LARRABEE

Then it's just as well you came up.

ALICE

I came to make sure—
(Glances about)

LARRABEE

Of what?

ALICE

You're going to swindle and deceive him—I know that. *Is there anything more?*
(Advancing to him a little)

LARRABEE

What could you do if there was?

ALICE

I could buy you off. Such men as you are always open to sale.

LARRABEE

How much would you give?

ALICE

The genuine package—the real ones. All the proofs—everything.

LARRABEE

(*Advancing R.C. above table, quietly but with quick interest*)

Have you got it with you?

ALICE

No, but I can get it.

LARRABEE

Oh—

(*Going to table. Slightly disappointed*)

So you'll do all that for this man? Would you? I suppose you think he's your friend?

ALICE

I haven't thought of it.

LARRABEE

Look what he's doing now. Coming here to buy those things off me.

ALICE

They're false. They're counterfeit.

LARRABEE

He thinks they're genuine, doesn't he? He'd hardly come here to buy them if he didn't.

ALICE

He *may* ask my permission still.

LARRABEE

(*Sneer—turning away*)

He won't get the chance.

ALICE

(*Suspicious again*)

He won't get the chance. Then there *is* something else.

LARRABEE

Something else!

(*Turning to her*)

Why, you see me here by myself, don't you? I'm just going to talk to him on a little business.

ALICE

(*Advancing to C.*)

Where are those men who came up here?

LARRABEE

What men?

(*R.C., R. of table*)

ALICE

Three villainous-looking men—I saw them go in at the street door—

LARRABEE

Oh—those men. They went up the other stairway.

(*Pointing over shoulder to up R.*)

You can see them in the next building—if you look through that window.

ALICE

(*Starting toward door L.*)

I'll look in the passageway, if you please.

LARRABEE

(*Taking one step down before door L., quietly*)

But I don't please.

ALICE

(*Stops before him*)

You wouldn't *dare* to keep me here.

LARRABEE

I might *dare*—but I won't. *You'd be in the way.*

ALICE

Where are those men?

(*Whistle*)

LARRABEE

Now you stay just where you are and you'll see them very soon.

ALICE

Oh, I knew it.

(*Moving back a step R.C. seeing from this that they are going to attack* HOLMES)

Ah!

(*Under breath. After slight pause she turns and hurries to window, trying to look out or give an alarm. Then runs to cupboard door.*

LARRABEE *stops her. Then she comes C., stops and stands looking at them.* LARRABEE *waits, watching her movements*)

ALICE (*Continued*)

(*Desperately*)

You're going to do him some harm.

LARRABEE

Oh no, it's just a little joke—at his expense.

ALICE

(*Moving toward him a little*)

Look, you wanted the letters, the package I had in the safe! I'll get it for you. Let me go and I'll bring it here—or whatever you tell me—

(LARRABEE *sneers meaningly*)

I won't say a word to anyone—not to him—not to the policemen —not *anyone!*

LARRABEE

(*Without moving*)

You needn't take the trouble to *get* it—but you *can tell me where it is*—and you better be quick about it too—

ALICE

(*C.*)

Yes—if you'll promise not to go on with this.

LARRABEE

(*L.C.*)

Of course! That's understood.

ALICE

(*Excitedly C.*)

You promise!

LARRABEE

(*L.C.*)

Certainly I promise. Now where is it?

ALICE

(*C.*)

It's just outside my bedroom window—just outside on the left, fastened between the shutter and the wall—you can easily find it.

LARRABEE

Yes—I can easily find it.

ALICE

Now tell them—tell them to go.

LARRABEE

(*Going down to L., to men*)

She mustn't get back to the house—not till I've been there. Tie her up, keep her outside.

(ALICE *listens dazed, astonished*)

CRAIGIN

(*Speaks low*)

Go an' get a hold, Leary. Hand me a piece of that rope.

(MC TAGUE *brings rope from under his coat. Business of getting rapidly ready to gag and tie* ALICE. *Much time must not be spent on this; quick, businesslike.* MC TAGUE *takes handerchief from pocket to use as gag.* ALICE *begins to move back in alarm and looking at* LARRABEE)

ALICE

You said—you said if I *told* you—

LARRABEE

Well—we haven't done him any harm yet, have we?

(LEARY *is moving quietly around behind her*)

ALICE

(*Up C. a little*)

Then send them away.

LARRABEE

(*Half back to audience, looking L.*)

Certainly. Go away now, boys, there's no more work for you to-night.

ALICE

(*Looking at them terrified*)

They don't obey you. They are—

(LEARY *seizes her. She screams and resists, but* CRAIGIN *and* MCTAGUE *come at once up C., so that she is quickly subdued and gagged with handkerchief, etc., and her hands tied. As the struggle takes place,* MEN *work up L.C. to near cupboard with* ALICE. LARRABEE *also eagerly watching them tie* ALICE *up. This is not prolonged more than is absolutely necessary. Just as they finish, a shrill whistle is heard in distance outside R. at back, as if from street far below. All stop—listening—picture*)

CRAIGIN

Now out of the door with her—

(*The prolonged shrill whistle is heard again*)

LARRABEE

By God, he's *here*.

CRAIGIN

What!

LARRABEE

That's Sid Prince, I put him on the watch.

CRAIGIN

We won't have time to get her out.

LARRABEE

Shut her in that cupboard.

(*Pointing to cupboard up L.C.*)

LEARY

Yes—that'll do.

CRAIGIN

In with her.

> (LEARY *and* CRAIGIN, *almost on the word, take her toward cupboard.* MCTAGUE *goes and keeps watch at door down L.*
>
> *As he holds* ALICE)

Open that door! Open that door! There's no lock on this 'ere door.

LARRABEE

No lock!

LEARY

No.

LARRABEE

Drive something in.

CRAIGIN

Here, this knife.

> (*Hands* LEARY *a large clasp-knife opened ready*)

LARRABEE

A knife won't hold it.

CRAIGIN

Yes it will. Drive it in strong.

> (LEARY *drives blade in door frame with all his force*)

LEARY

'E'll have to find us 'ere.

CRAIGIN

Yes—and he won't either—we'll go and do 'im up.

> (*Going to door down L.*)

LARRABEE

No, you won't.

(*Men stop. Pause*)

I'll see him first, if you please.

CRAIGIN

Why you . . .

(CRAIGIN *and* LARRABEE *facing each other savagely an instant well downstage*)

McTAGUE

Them was orders, Craigin.

LEARY

So it was.

McTAGUE

There might be time to get back in the passage.

(*He listens at door L. and cautiously looks off—turns back into room*)

He ain't gone up one flight yet.

(*Exit* McTAGUE *at door L.,* LEARY *and* CRAIGIN. *Door does not close.* LARRABEE *glances at door up L.C. anxiously. Makes a quick dash up to it, and forces knife in with all his strength. Comes quickly down R. of table, pulls off coat and hat, throwing them on boxes R., and sits quietly chewing an end of cigar.*

Enter SHERLOCK HOLMES *at door L., walking easily as though on some ordinary business.*

Stop music)

HOLMES

(*Seeing the apartment with a glance as he enters and pausing L.C., disappointed. His little laugh, with no smile*)

How the devil is it that crooks always hit on the same places for their dubious business?

(*Chuckles of amusement*)

Well! I certainly thought, after driving about for exactly an hour in a closed cab you'd show me something new.

LARRABEE

(*Looking up nonchalantly*)

Seen it before, have you?

HOLMES

(*Standing still L.C.*)

Well, I should think I have.

(*Moves easily about recalling dear old times*)

I nabbed a friend of yours in here once; he was trying to drop himself out of that window. Ned Colvin, cracksman.

LARRABEE

Colvin. I never heard of him before.

HOLMES

No? Well, you never heard of him after. A brace of counter-feiters used these regal chambers in the spring of ninety. One of them hid in the cupboard.

LARRABEE

Times have changed since then.

(HOLMES *darts a lightning glance at* LARRABEE. *Instantly easy again and glancing about as before*)

HOLMES

(*Dropping down near* LARRABEE)

So they have, Mr. Larrabee—so they have.

(*A little confidentially*)

Then it was only cracksmen, counterfeiters, petty swindlers of various kinds. Now—

    (*Pause, looking at* LARRABEE.

    LARRABEE *turns and looks at* HOLMES)

LARRABEE

What now?

HOLMES

    (*Mysteriously*)

Between you and me, Mr. Larrabee—we've heard some not altogether agreeable rumors; rumors of some pretty shady work not too far from here—a murder or two of an almost inexplicable kind—and I've got a suspicion—

    (*Stops. Sniffs very delicately. Motionless pause. Nods ominously to* LARRABEE, *who is looking about, and gets over toward window. When within reach, he runs his hand lightly along the frame*)

My surmise is correct—it is.

    (*Coming C.*)

LARRABEE

    (*Turning to* HOLMES)

It is what?

HOLMES

Caulked.

    (*Above table*)

LARRABEE

What does that signify to us?

HOLMES

Nothing to us, Mr. Larrabee, nothing to us. It could signify a good deal to some poor devil who got himself caught in this trap.

LARRABEE

Well, if it's nothing to us, suppose we leave it alone and get to business. My time is limited.

HOLMES

Quite so, I should have realized that these reflections could not possibly appeal to you.

(*Standing a little above* LARRABEE)

But I take a deep interest in all that pertains to what are known as the criminal classes. This same interest makes me very anxious to learn

(*Looking straight at* LARRABEE, *who looks up at him*)

—how you happened to choose this rather gruesome place for an ordinary business transaction.

(*Stands L. of table*)

LARRABEE

(*Looking at* HOLMES *across the table*)

I chose this place, Mr. Holmes, because I thought you might not be disposed to take such liberties here as you practiced in my own house last night.

HOLMES

(*Looks innocently at* LARRABEE)

Why not?

(*They look at one another an instant*)

LARRABEE

(*Significantly*)

You might not feel quite so much at home.

HOLMES

(*A little laugh*)

There you make a singular miscalculation, Mr. Larrabee. I feel perfectly at home, Mr. Larrabee! Perfectly!

(He seats himself at table in languid and leisurely manner, takes cigar from packet, and lights it)

LARRABEE

(Looks at him an instant.

LARRABEE *now takes out the counterfeit package of papers, etc., and tosses it on the table before them.*

HOLMES *looks on floor L. slightly by light of match, unobserved by* LARRABEE*)*

Here is the little packet which is the object of this meeting.

(He glances at HOLMES *to see effect of its production)*

*(*HOLMES *looks at it calmly as he smokes)*

LARRABEE *(Continued)*

I haven't opened it yet, but Miss Faulkner assures me everything is there.

HOLMES

Then there is no need of opening it, Mr. Larrabee.

LARRABEE

I want to see you satisfied.

HOLMES

That is precisely the condition in which you now behold me. Miss Faulkner is a truthful young lady. Her word is sufficient.

LARRABEE

Very well. Now what shall we say, Mr. Holmes?

(Pause)

Course, we're asking a pretty large price for this. I mean Miss Faulkner is giving up everything. She wouldn't be satisfied unless the result justified it.

HOLMES

(*Pointedly*)

Suppose, Mr. Larrabee, that as Miss Faulkner knows nothing whatever about this affair, we omit her name from the discussion.

LARRABEE

Who said she knows nothing?

HOLMES

You did. Every look, tone, gesture—everything you have said and done since I have entered this room informs me that she has never consented to this transaction. This is a little speculation of your own.

LARRABEE

I suppose you think you can read me like a book.

HOLMES

No, like a primer.

LARRABEE

Ha! Well, let that pass. How much'll you give?

HOLMES

One thousand pounds.

LARRABEE

I couldn't take it.

HOLMES

What do you ask?

LARRABEE

Five thousand.

HOLMES

(*Shakes head*)

I couldn't give it.

LARRABEE

Very well, Mr. Holmes.

(*Rises*)

In that case, we've had all this trouble for nothing.

(*As if about to put up the packet*)

HOLMES

(*Leaning back in chair and remonstrating*)

Oh—please don't say that, Mr. Larrabee! To me the occasion has
been doubly interesting. I've not only had the pleasure of meeting you again, but I have also availed myself of the opportunity
of making some observations regarding this place which may not
come amiss.

(LARRABEE *looks at* HOLMES *contemptuously. He
places chair under table*)

LARRABEE

Why, I've been offered four thousand for that little lot.

HOLMES

Why didn't you take it?

LARRABEE

Because I intend to get more.

HOLMES

That's too bad.

LARRABEE

If they offered four thousand they'll give five.

HOLMES

On the contrary. They won't give anything.

LARRABEE

Why not?

HOLMES

Because they've turned the case over to me.

LARRABEE

Will you give me three thousand?

HOLMES

(*Rising*)

Strange as may appear, Mr. Larrabee, my time is quite as limited as yours. I have brought with me the sum of one thousand pounds. That is all I intend to pay. If it is your desire to sell at that figure kindly apprise me of the fact at once. No?—permit me to wish you a very good evening.

(*Pause.* LARRABEE *looks at him*)

LARRABEE

(*After the pause glances nervously around up L. once, fearing he heard something*)

Oh, go on!

(*Tosses packet on table*)

You can have it. It's too small a matter to haggle over.

(HOLMES *reseats himself at once, back of table, and takes wallet from his pocket, from which he produces a bunch of bank notes.* LARRABEE *stands down R. a little, watching him with glittering eye.* HOLMES *counts out ten one-hundred-pound notes and lays the remainder of the notes on the table at his R. with elbow on them, while he counts the first over again*)

LARRABEE

(*Sneeringly*)

I thought you said you had brought just a thousand.

HOLMES

(*Not looking up; counting the notes*)

I did. This is it.

LARRABEE

You brought a trifle more, I see.

HOLMES

(*Counting notes*)

I didn't say I hadn't brought any more.

LARRABEE

(*Sneers*)

You can do your little tricks when it comes to it, can't you?

HOLMES

Well, that depends on whom I'm dealing with.

(*Hands* LARRABEE *one thousand pounds in notes.*

LARRABEE *takes money and keeps a close watch at same time on the remaining pile of notes lying at* HOLMES'S *L.* HOLMES, *after handing the notes to* LARRABEE, *lays cigar he was smoking on the table, picks up packet which he puts in his pocket, with his right hand, and is almost at the same time reaching with his left hand for the notes he placed upon the table when* LARRABEE *makes a sudden lunge and snatches the pile of bank notes, jumping back to R. on the instant.* HOLMES *springs to his feet at the same time*)

HOLMES (*Continued*)

Now I've got you where I want you, Jim Larrabee! You've been very cunning, very cautious, very wise, there was nothing to hold you for—but that little slip will get you ten years for *robbery*—

LARRABEE

(*At R.*)

Oh! You'll have me in, will you?

(*Short, sneering laugh*)

What are your views about being able to get away from here yourself?

HOLMES

I do not anticipate any particular difficulty.

LARRABEE

(*Significantly*)

You might change your mind about that.

HOLMES

Whether I change my mind or not, I certainly shall leave this place, and your arrest will swiftly follow.

LARRABEE

My arrest? Ha, ha! Robbery, eh—why, even if you got away from here you haven't got a witness. Not a witness to your *name*.

HOLMES

(*Slowly backing up C., keeping his eyes sharply on* LARRABEE *as he does so*)

I'm not so sure of that, Mr. Larrabee!— *Do you usually fasten* this door with *a knife?*

LARRABEE

Come away from that door.

(*But* HOLMES *has the door torn open and* ALICE FAULKNER *out before* LARRABEE *gets near*)

HOLMES

Stand back!

(Turning to LARRABEE, *supporting* ALICE *at same time)*

You contemptible scoundrel!

(Untying ALICE *quickly)*

I'm afraid you're badly hurt, Miss Faulkner.

(Enter CRAIGIN *at door L. He stands there a moment near door watching* HOLMES. *He makes a signal with hand to others outside door and then moves noiselessly to L.C.* MC TAGUE *enters at door L., noiselessly, and remains a little behind* CRAIGIN *below door L.* ALICE *shakes her head quickly, thinking of what she sees, and tries to call* HOLMES's *attention to* CRAIGIN *and* MC TAGUE)

ALICE

No!—Mr. Holmes.

(Pointing to CRAIGIN *and* MC TAGUE)

HOLMES

(Glances around)

Ah, Craigin—delighted to see you.

*(*CRAIGIN *gives slight start)*

And you too, Mc Tague. I infer from your presence here at this particular jucture that I am not dealing with Mr. Larrabee *alone.*

LARRABEE

(Standing at R. half down)

Your inference is quite correct, Mr. Holmes.

HOLMES

It is not difficult to imagine who is at the bottom of such a conspiracy as this.

(CRAIGIN *begins to steal across to R. noiselessly.*
MC TAGUE *remains before door L. Holmes turns to*
ALICE *again*)

I hope you're beginning to feel more yourself, Miss Faulkner—
because we shall leave here very soon.

ALICE

(*Who has been shrinking from the sight of* CRAIGIN
and MC TAGUE)

Oh yes—please do let us go.

CRAIGIN

(*Low, deep voice, intense, R.C. below table*)

You'll 'ave to wait a bit, Mr. 'Olmes. We have a little matter of
business we'd like to talk over.

(HOLMES *turning R.C. to* CRAIGIN.

Enter LEARY *at door L., and glides up L. side in the
shadow and begins to move toward* HOLMES *from up
L. In approaching from corner up L. he glides behind
door of cupboard up L.C. as it stands swung open, and
from there down on* HOLMES *at cue. As* HOLMES *turns
to* CRAIGIN, ALICE *leans against wall of cupboard L.C.*)

HOLMES

Very well, Craigin, I'll see you tomorrow morning in your cell at
Bow Street.

CRAIGIN

(*Threateningly*)

Werry sorry, sir, but I cawn't wait till morning. It's got to be set-
tled tonight.

HOLMES

(*Looks at* CRAIGIN *an instant and coming down C. a
step or two*)

Oh, very well, Craigin, we'll settle it tonight.

CRAIGIN

It's so werry himportant, Mr. 'Olmes—so werry himportant indeed *that you'll 'ave to 'tend to it now.*

(*At this instant* ALICE *sees* LEARY *approaching rapidly from behind and screams.* HOLMES *turns, but* LEARY *is upon him at the same time. There is a very short struggle, and* HOLMES *throws* LEARY *violently off to L. but* LEARY *has got* HOLMES's *revolver. As they struggle,* ALICE *steps back to side of room upstage. A short, deadly pause.* LARRABEE *comes down R.* HOLMES *motionless a little up C. regarding the men.* ALICE *up back against wall.* CRAIGIN *facing him motionless from downstage R.C. After the pause* LEARY *begins to revive*)

CRAIGIN

(*Low voice to* LEARY)

'Ave you got his revolver?

LEARY

(*Showing revolver*)

'Ere it is.

(*Getting slowly to his feet*)

HOLMES

(*Recognizing* LEARY *in the dim light*)

Ah, Leary!

(*Up C.*)

It needed only your blithe personality to make the party complete.

(*Sits and writes rapidly on pocket pad at table R.C. pushing lamp away a little and picking up cigar which he had left on the table, and which he keeps in his mouth as he writes*)

HOLMES (*Continued*)

There is only one other I could wish to welcome here, and that is the talented author of this midnight carnival. I shall have him, however, by tomorrow night.

CRAIGIN

(*R.C.*)

Though 'e ain't 'ere, Mr. 'Olmes, 'e gave me a message for yer. 'E presented his koindest compliments and wished yer a pleasant trip across.

HOLMES

(*Writing—cigar in mouth*)

That's very kind of him, I'm sure.

(*Writes*)

LARRABEE

(*Sneeringly*)

Writing your will, are you?

HOLMES

(*Writing—with quick glances at the rest*)

No.

(*Shakes head*)

Just a brief description of one or two of you gentlemen—for the police. They know the others.

LEARY

And when will you give it 'em, Mr. 'Olmes?

HOLMES

(*Writes*)

In nine or nine and a half minutes, Mr. Leary.

LARRABEE

You leaving here in nine minutes, are you?

HOLMES

No.

(*Writing*)

In one. It will take me eight minutes to find a policeman. This is a very dangerous neighborhood.

LARRABEE

Well, when you're ready to start, let us know.

HOLMES

(*Rising and putting pad in pocket*)

I'm ready now.

(*Buttoning up coat.*

CRAIGIN, MC TAGUE, *and* LEARY *suddenly brace themselves for action, and stand ready to make a run for* HOLMES. LARRABEE *also is ready to join in the struggle if necessary, down R.* HOLMES *moves backward from table a little to* ALICE—*she drops down a step toward* HOLMES)

CRAIGIN

I've an idea you won't be going anywhere, Mr. 'Olmes, cause we're goin' to tie yer down nice and tight to the top o' that table.

HOLMES

By Jove! . . . don't think you *will*, you know. That's my idea.

CRAIGIN

An' you'll save yourself a deal of trouble if ye submit quiet and easy like—because if ye don't ye moight get knocked about a bit—

ALICE

(*Under her breath*)

Oh—Mr. Holmes!

(*Coming closer to* HOLMES)

LARRABEE

(*To* ALICE)

Come away from him! Stay over here if you don't want to get hurt.

(*Love music*)

HOLMES

(*To* ALICE, *without looking around, but reaching her with left hand*)

If you don't want to get hurt, my child, stay close to me.

(ALICE *moves closer to* HOLMES)

LARRABEE

Aren't you coming?

ALICE

(*Breathlessly*)

No!

CRAIGIN

You'd better look out, miss—he might get killed.

ALICE

Then you can kill me too.

(HOLMES *makes a quick turn to her, with sudden exclamation under breath. For an instant only he looks in her face—then a quick turn back to* CRAIGIN *and men*)

HOLMES

(*Low voice—not taking eyes from men before him*)

I'm afraid you don't mean that, Miss Faulkner.

ALICE

(*Still above him on his L.*)

Yes, I *do*.

HOLMES

(*Eyes on men—though they shift about rapidly, but never toward* ALICE)

No.

(*Shakes head a trifle*)

You would not say it—at another time or place.

ALICE

I would say it anywhere—always.

(*Music stops*)

CRAIGIN

So you'll 'ave it out with us, eh?

HOLMES

Did you suppose for one moment, Craigin, that I wouldn't, Craigin?

CRAIGIN

Well, then—I'll 'ave to give you one—same as I did yer right-'and man this afternoon.

(*Approaching* HOLMES)

HOLMES

(*To* ALICE *without turning—intense, rapid*)

Ah!

(CRAIGIN *stops dead*)

You heard him say that. *Same as he did my right-hand man this afternoon.*

ALICE

(*Under breath*)

Yes! Yes!

HOLMES

However unpleasant the experience, I ask you to remember that face.

(*Pointing to* CRAIGIN)

In three days I shall ask you to identify it in the prisoner's dock.

(*Turning away as if to hide his face*)

HOLMES (*Continued*)

(*Very sharp—rapid*)

Yes—and the rest of you gentlemen with him. You surprise me, —thinking you're sure of anybody in this room, and never once taking the trouble to look at that window. If you wanted to make it perfectly safe, you should have had those *missing bars put back.*

(HOLMES *whispers something to* ALICE, *indicating her to make for door down L.*

Music till end of Act.

CRAIGIN, LEARY, MC TAGUE, LARRABEE *make very slight move and say "Eh?" but instantly at tension again, and all motionless, ready to spring on* HOLMES. HOLMES *and* ALICE *motionless facing them. This is held an instant*)

LARRABEE

Bars or no bars, you're not going to get out of here as easy as you expect.

(HOLMES *moves easily down near table R.C.*)

HOLMES

There are so many ways, Mr. Larrabee, I hardly know which to choose.

CRAIGIN

(*Louder—advancing*)

Well, you'd better choose quick—I can tell you that.

HOLMES

(*Sudden—strong—sharp*)

I'll choose at once, Mr. Craigin—and my choice—

(*Quickly seizing the chair*)

—falls on this.

(*On the word he brings the chair down upon the lamp with a frightful crash, extinguishing light instantly. Every light out. Only the glow of* HOLMES's *cigar remains visible where he stands at the table. He at once begins to move up C. toward window, keeping cigar so that it will show to men and to front*)

CRAIGIN

(*Loud, sharp voice to others*)

The cigar. Trace 'im by the cigar.

(*Moving at once toward window up C.*)

Follow the cigar.

LARRABEE

(*Remaining down R.*)

Look out. He's going for the window.

(LEARY *goes quickly to window.* MC TAGUE *goes R. and is ready by safety lamp.* HOLMES *quickly fixes cigar in a crack or joint at side of window up R.C. so that it is still seen—smash of the window glass is heard. In-*

*stantly glides across L., well upstage, and down L. side
to the door L., where he finds* ALICE. *On crash of window* CRAIGIN *and* LEARY *give a quick shout of exclamation—they spring upstage toward the light of cigar
—sound of quick scuffle and blows up R. in darkness*)

LARRABEE

Get that light.

CRAIGIN

(*Clear and distinct*)

The safety lamp. Where is it?

(*Make this shout for lantern very strong and audible
to front.*

MC TAGUE *kicks over box which concealed the safety
lamp—lights up.* HOLMES *and* ALICE *at door L.* ALICE
just going out at L.)

HOLMES

(*Turning at door L., and pointing to window up C.*)

You'll find that cigar in a crevice by the window.

(*All start toward* HOLMES *with exclamations, oaths,
etc. He makes quick exit with* ALICE *at door L. and
slams it after him. Sounds of heavy bolts outside L.
sliding quickly into place, and heavy bars dropping
into position.* CRAIGIN, MC TAGUE, *and* LEARY *rush
against door and make violent efforts to open it. After
the first excited effort they turn quickly back to C. As*
MC TAGUE *crosses, he throws safety lamp on table R.C.*

LARRABEE, *who has stopped near C. when he saw door
closed, turns front with a look of hatred on his face
and mad with rage*)

CURTAIN

Scene 2

DR. WATSON's *house in Kensington. The consulting room. Oak paneling. Solid furniture. Wide double doors on R. opening to the hall and street door. Door up L. communicating with doctor's inner medicine room. A door in flat up C. a little to R. which opens to private hallway of house. The windows on L. side are supposed to open at side of house upon an area which faces the street. These windows have shades or blinds on rollers which can quickly be drawn down. At the opening of the Act they are down, so that no one could see into the room from the street.*

There is a large operating chair up R.C. with high back, cushions, etc.

Music for curtain, which stops an instant before rise.

DR. WATSON *is seated behind his desk L.C and* MRS. SMEEDLEY, *a seedy-looking, middle-aged woman, is seated in the chair C. and R. of the desk with a medicine bottle in her hand.*

MRS. SMEEDLEY

Thank you very much for seeing me, Doctor, it's very kind indeed.

WATSON

What ever you do, don't make any mistake about the medicine.

MRS. SMEEDLEY

Oh no I won't. Would you hold that, please. Green for 'er cough and brown for the fever.

WATSON

That's right. If she's no better tomorrow you will let me know, of course.

MRS. SMEEDLEY

Oh yes, Doctor, I'll come myself.

WATSON

And whatever you do, don't let her out.

MRS. SMEEDLEY

Oh no, Doctor, the fog 'ud kill her.

WATSON

Good night, Mrs. Smeedley.

MRS. SMEEDLEY

Good night, Doctor, thank you very much, Doctor. Good night, Doctor.

> (MRS. SMEEDLEY *exits at door R. Sound of door closing heard after she is off.*
>
> *Pause. The* DOCTOR *turns to his desk, and, ringing bell, then buries himself with papers.*
>
> *Enter* PARSONS—*a servant—at door R.*)

WATSON

Parsons!

> (PARSONS *comes a little toward* WATSON. *Lower voice*)

That woman who just left—do you know her?

PARSONS

> (*Trying to recollect*)

I can't say as I recollect 'avin' see 'er before. Was there anything—?

WATSON

Oh no! Acted a little strange, that's all. I thought I saw her looking about the hall before she went out.

PARSONS

Yes sir, she did give a look. I saw that myself, sir.

WATSON

(*After an instant's thought*)

Oh well—I daresay it was nothing. Is there anyone waiting, Parsons?

PARSONS

There's one person in the waiting room, sir—a gentleman.

WATSON

(*Looks at watch*)

I'll see him, but I've only a short time left.

PARSONS

Very well, sir. I'll show the gentlemen in, sir?

WATSON

Yes, if you would.

(PARSONS *exits at door R. Short pause.* WATSON *busy at desk.* PARSONS *opens door R. and shows in* SID PRINCE. *He comes in a little way and pauses.* PARSONS *all through this Act closes the door R. after his exit, or after showing anyone in.* WATSON *looks up*)

PRINCE

(*Speaking in the most dreadful husky whisper at L.C.*)

Good evenin', Doctor!

WATSON

Good evening.

(*Indicating chair C.*)

Pray, be seated.

PRINCE

(*Same voice all through*)

Thanks, I don't mind if I do.

(*Coughs, then sits in chair up C. near desk on* WATSON's *R.*)

WATSON

(*Looking at him with professional interest*)

Well, what seems to be the trouble?

PRINCE

Throat, sir.

(*Indicating his throat to assist in making himself understood*)

It's a sore throat. The fog.

WATSON

Sore throat, eh?

(*Glancing about for an instrument*)

PRINCE

Yes. It's the most 'arrowing thing I ever 'ad! It pains me that much to swallow that I—

WATSON

Hurts you to swallow, does it?

(*Finding and picking up an instrument on the desk*)

PRINCE

Indeed it does. Why, I can 'ardly force a bit of food down 'cept for little tiddly morsels, an' a spot of calf's-foot jelly.

(WATSON *rises and goes to cabinet up L.C., pushes gas burner out into position and lights it*)

WATSON

Well, just relax one moment. Please.

(PRINCE *rises and goes up on* WATSON'S *R.* WATSON *adjusts reflector over eye, etc. He has an instrument in his hand which he wipes with a napkin*)

Now, mouth open—wide as possible.

(PRINCE *opens mouth and* WATSON *places tongue holder on his tongue. Picks up dentist's mirror and warms it over gas burner—business.*

WATSON *is about to examine throat when* PRINCE *sees instrument and is a trifle alarmed.*

Business of WATSON *putting in tongue holder and looking down* PRINCE'S *throat—looking carefully this way and that*)

WATSON

Say "Ah!"

PRINCE

(*Husky voice*)

Ah!

(*Steps away to R. and places handkerchief to mouth as if the attempt to say "Ah!" hurt him.*)

WATSON

Again?

PRINCE

Ah!

(WATSON *discontinues, and takes instrument out of* PRINCE's *mouth*)

WATSON

(*A slight incredulity in his manner*)

Where exactly do you feel this pain?

PRINCE

(*Indicating with his finger*)

Just about there, Doctor, 'orrible. Inside about there.

WATSON

That's odd. I don't find anything wrong.

(*Pushes gas burner back to usual position—and placing instrument on cabinet*)

PRINCE

You may not foind it wrong, but I feel it wrong. If you would only give me something to take away this awful agony. Pain, pain, nothin' but pain.

WATSON

(*Reflectively*)

Singular it should have affected your voice in this way. Well, I'll give you a gargle—it may help you a little.

PRINCE

Yes—if you only would, Doctor.

WATSON

What are you doing there?

PRINCE

Why, nothing at all, Doctor. I felt such a draft on the back o' my neck don't yer know, that I opened the door to see where it came from!

(WATSON *goes down and rings bell on his desk, placing bottle on papers. Pause. Enter* PARSONS *at door R.*)

PRINCE

Parsons!

WATSON

Parsons, show this man the shortest way to the street door and close the door after him.

PRINCE

But, Doctor, ye don't understand.

WATSON

I understand quite enough. Good evening.

PRINCE

Yer know, the draft plays hell with my throat, sir—I get this terrible shooting experience.

WATSON

Good evening.

(*He sits and pays no further attention to* PRINCE)

PARSONS

This way, sir, if you please.

PRINCE

I consider that you've treated me damned outrageous, that's wot I do, and ye won't hear the last of this very soon.

(PARSONS *has forced* PRINCE *out by the arm at door R. during foregoing speech. Door closes after* PRINCE *R. Sound of outside door closing follows shortly, outside R.* WATSON, *after short pause, looks around room, not observing that window shades are up. He rings bell. Enter* PARSONS *at door R.*)

WATSON

(*Rises and gathers up a few things as if to go*)

I shall be at Mr. Holmes's in Baker Street. If there's anything special, you'll know where to send for me. The appointment was for nine.

(*Looks at watch*)

It's fifteen minutes past eight now—I'm going to walk over.

(*Door bell of outside door rings*)

No. I won't see any more tonight.

PARSONS

Yes, sir.

(*He starts toward door R. to answer bell.*
WATSON *looks L. and sees blinds up*)

WATSON

Parsons!

(PARSONS *turns*)

Why aren't those blinds down?

PARSONS

They was down, sir, only a few moments ago, sir!

WATSON

That's strange! Well, you'd better pull them down now.

PARSONS

Yes, sir.

(*Bell rings twice as* PARSONS *pulls second blind down.
He exits R. to answer bell. Pause. Then enter* PARSONS
at door R. in a peculiar manner)

WATSON

You'd better go see who it is!

PARSONS

Yes sir. If you please, sir, it isn't a patient at all, sir.

WATSON

Well, what is it?

PARSONS

A lady, sir—

> (WATSON *looks up*)

—and she wants to see you most particular, sir!

WATSON

What does she want to see me about?

PARSONS

She didn't say, sir. Only she said it was of the hutmost himportance, if you could see 'er, sir.

WATSON

Is she there in the hall?

PARSONS

Yes, sir.

WATSON

Very well—I was going to walk for the exercise, but I suppose I can take a cab.

PARSONS

Then you'll see the lady, sir.

WATSON

Yes. Show her in.

> (PARSONS *turns to go*. WATSON *continues his preparations*)

WATSON (*Continued*)

And call a cab for me at the same time—have it wait.

Yes, sir.

> (PARSONS *exits at door R. Pause.* PARSONS *appears at door R. ushering in a lady—and exits when she has entered.*
>
> *Enter* MADGE LARRABEE *at door R. Her manner is entirely different from that of the former scenes. She is an impetuous, gushing society lady, with trouble on her mind*)

MADGE

> (*As she comes in*)

Ah! Doctor—it's awfully good of you to see me. I know what a busy man you must be—I'm in such trouble—Doctor, oh, it's really too dreadful—you'll forgive my troubling you in this way, won't you?

WATSON

Don't speak of it, madam.

MADGE

Oh, thank you so much! It did look frightful my coming in like that—but I'm not alone—oh no! —I left my maid in the cab— I'm Mrs. H. de Witte Seaton—

> (*Trying to find cardcase*)

Dear me—I didn't bring my cardcase—or if I did, I lost it.

WATSON

Don't trouble with a card, Mrs. Seaton.

> (*With gesture to indicate chair up C.*)

MADGE

Thank you so much.

> (*Sitting as she continues to talk*)

You don't know what I've been through this evening—trying to find some one who could tell me what to do.

(WATSON *sits in chair at desk*)

It's something that happened, Doctor—it just simply happened —I know it wasn't his fault! I know it!

WATSON

Whose fault?

MADGE

My brother's—my poor, dear, youngest brother—he couldn't possibly have done such a thing, he simply couldn't and—

WATSON

Such a thing as what, Mrs. Seaton?

MADGE

As to take the plans of our naval defenses at Gibraltar from the Admiralty offices. They think he stole them, Doctor—and they've arrested him for it—you see, he works there. He was the only person who knew anything about them in the whole office— because they trusted him so. He was to make copies and—oh,

(*Overcome, she takes out her handkerchief and wipes her eyes. This must all be perfectly natural, and not in the least particular overdone*)

WATSON

I'm terribly sorry, Mrs. Seaton—

MADGE

(*Mixed up with sobs*)

Oh, thank you so much! They told me you were Mr. Holmes's friend—several people told me that, several—they advised me to ask you where I could find him—and everything depends on it, Doctor—everything.

WATSON

Holmes, of course. He's just the one you want.

MADGE

Yes, that's it! He's just the one—and there's very little time left! They'll take my poor brother away to prison tomorrow!

(*Shows signs of breaking down again*)

WATSON

There, there, Mrs. Seaton—pray control yourself.

MADGE

(*Choking down sobs*)

Now what would you advise me to do?

WATSON

Well, I would go to Mr. Holmes at once.

MADGE

But I've been. I've been, and he wasn't *there!*

WATSON

You went to his house?

MADGE

Yes—in Baker Street. That's why I came to you! They told me he might be here!

WATSON

No—he isn't here!

(*Turns away slightly.*

MADGE *looks deeply discouraged*)

MADGE

But don't you expect him some time this evening?

WATSON

No.

(Shaking head)

There's no possibility of his coming—so far as I know.

MADGE

But couldn't you *get* him to come?

(Pause)

It would be such a great favor to me—I'm almost worn out with going about—in this anxiety! If you could get word to him to—

(Sees that WATSON *is looking at her strangely and sharply)*

—to come.

(Brief pause)

WATSON

(Rising—rather hard voice)

No, I could *not* get him to come. And I beg you to excuse me. I am going out myself—

(Looks at watch)

—on urgent business.

(Rings bell)

MADGE

(Rising)

Oh, certainly! Don't let me detain you! And you think I had better call at his house again?

WATSON

(Coldly)

That will be the wisest thing to do.

MADGE

Oh, thank you so much.

(Extends her hand)

You don't *know* how you've encouraged me!

(WATSON *withdraws his hand, as he still looks at her.
Enter* PARSONS *at door R. He stands at door*)

MADGE (*Continued*)

Well—good night, Doctor.

(WATSON *simply bows coldly.* MADGE *turns to go. The
crash of a capsizing vehicle, followed by excited shouts
of men, is heard. This effect must be as if outside the
house with doors closed, and not close at hand.* MADGE
stops suddenly on hearing the crash, and shouts.
WATSON *looks at* PARSONS)

WATSON

What's that, Parsons?

PARSONS

I really can't say, sir, but it sounded to me like a haccident.

MADGE

(*Turning to* WATSON *near C.*)

Oh *dear!* I do hope it isn't anything serious!

WATSON

Probably nothing more serious than a broken-down cab. See
what it is, Parsons.

(*Bell and knock at R.* MADGE *turns and looks toward
door again, anxiously.* PARSONS *turns to go. Sudden
vigorous ringing of door bell outside R., followed by
the sound of a knocker violently used*)

PARSONS

There's the bell, sir! There's somebody 'urt, sir, an' they're
a-wantin' *you!*

WATSON

Well, don't allow anybody to come in!

(Looks at watch)

I have no more time.

(Hurriedly gathers papers up)

PARSONS

Very well, sir.

(Exit at door R., leaving door open.

MADGE *turns from looking off at door, and looks at*
WATSON *anxiously. Looks toward door again.*

*Sounds of voices outside R. Following speeches outside
are not in rotation, but jumbled together, so that it is
all over very quickly)*

FIRST VOICE

(Outside)

We 'ad to bring 'im in, man. There's nowhere else to go!

PARSONS

(Outside)

The doctor can't see anybody.

SECOND VOICE

(Outside)

Well, let the old gent lay 'ere awhile, can't yer. It's common de-
cency. Wot 'ave yer got a red lamp 'angin' outsider yer bloomin'
door for?

MADGE

But they're coming *in*, Doctor.

(Retreats backward up L.C. until a little above from
WATSON)

WATSON

(Moving toward door R.)

Parsons! Parsons!

(MADGE *watches from up L.C.*

Enter PARSONS *at door R. Door closes and noise stops*)

PARSONS

They would bring 'im in, sir. It's an old gentleman as was 'urt a bit w'en the cab upset!

MADGE

(*Up L.C.*)

Oh!

(*Sounds of groans, etc., outside L., and the old* GEN-TLEMAN *whining out complaints and threats*)

WATSON

Let them put him here.

(*Indicating operating chair up R.*)

Have that cab wait for me.

PARSONS

Yes, sir!

WATSON

Help him in, Parsons.

(PARSONS *exits at door R.*)

MADGE

Oh, Doctor, isn't it frightful.

WATSON

(*Turning to door up C.*)

Mrs. Seaton, if you will be so good as to step this way, you can reach the street by taking the first door to your left.

MADGE

(*Hesitating*)

But I—I may be of some help, Doctor.

WATSON

(*With a trifle of impatience*)

None whatever.

(*Holds door open*)

MADGE

But, Doctor—I *must see* the poor fellow—I haven't the *power* to go!

WATSON

(*Facing* MADGE *up C.*)

Madam, I believe you have some ulterior motive in coming here! You will kindly—

(*Enter at door R. a white-haired old* GENTLEMAN *in black clerical clothes, white tie, etc., assisted by* PAR-SONS *on R. side and the* DRIVER *on L. He limps as though his leg were hurt. His coat is soiled. His hat is soiled as if it had rolled in the street.* MADGE *has retired up L. above desk, and watches old* GENTLEMAN *closely from there without moving.* WATSON *turns toward the party as they come in*)

HOLMES

(*As he comes in*)

Oh, oh!

(*He limps so that he hardly touches his right foot to floor*)

PARSONS

(*As he helps* HOLMES *in*)

This way, sir! Be careful of the step, sir!—Mind your leg, sir. Up we go. That's it. (*etc.*)

DRIVER

(*As he comes in, and also beginning outside before entrance*)

Now we'll go in 'ere. You'll see the doctor an' it'll be all right.

HOLMES

No, it won't be all right.

PARSONS

Now over to this chair.

(*Indicating chair R.C.*)

HOLMES

(*Pushing back and trying to stop at the chair down R.*)

No, I'll sit here.

PARSONS

No, this is the chair, sir.

HOLMES

Don't I know where I want to sit!

DRIVER

(*Impatiently*)

You'll sit 'ere.

(*They lead him up to chair R.C. As they lead him up*)

Now, the doctor'll have a look at ye. That's the doctor.

HOLMES

That's not a doctor.

DRIVER

That is a doctor.

(*Seeing* WATSON *over near C.*)

HOLMES

(*Still standing back to audience and turning to* DRIVER
on his L.)

Are you the driver?

DRIVER

Yes, I'm the driver.

HOLMES

Well, I'll have you arrested for this.

DRIVER

You cawn't arrest me.

HOLMES

No, I can't but somebody else can. You are very disagreeable
man!

(*The* DRIVER *is trying to talk back and make* HOLMES
sit down. HOLMES *turns suddenly on* PARSONS *on his
R.* WATSON *is trying to attract* PARSONS' *attention*)

Are you a driver?

PARSONS

No, sir!

HOLMES

Well, what are you?

PARSONS

I'm the butler, sir.

HOLMES

Butler! Butler! A likely story.

DRIVER

He's the doctor's servant.

HOLMES

Who asked you who he was?

DRIVER

Never mind who asked me—I'm telling you.

HOLMES

Well, go and tell somebody else.

DRIVER

(*Trying to push* HOLMES *into chair*)

Sit down here! Sit down and be quiet.

WATSON

(*To* PARSONS)

Parsons, see that that cab is waiting for me. I better take a look at him.

PARSONS

Yes, sir.

(*Exits*)

HOLMES

(*Resisting*)

Quiet! Quiet! Where's my hat? My hat! My hat!

DRIVER

There's your 'at in your 'and.

HOLMES

(*Looks at hat*)

Oh, no . . . you'd better give it up to the poor.

(*As* DRIVER *is trying to push him into chair*)—

You're responsible.

(*In chair*)

I'll have you arrested.

(*Clinging to* DRIVER's *coat tail as he tries to get away to door R.*)

Here, come back.

(*Choking with rage*)

DRIVER

(*First wrenching away coat from* HOLMES's *grasp; at door down R.*)

I cawn't stay around 'ere, you know! Some one'll be pinching my cab.

(*Exit* DRIVER *R.*)

HOLMES

(*Screaming after him*)

Then bring your cab in here. I want—

(*Lapses into groans and remonstrances*)

Why didn't somebody stop him? These cabmen! What did he bring me in here for? I know where I am, it's a conspiracy. I won't stay in this place. If I ever get out of here alive—(*etc.*)

WATSON

(*Steps quickly to door R., speaking off*)

Parsons—take that man's number.

(*Quickly to old* GENTLEMAN)

Now, sir, if you'll sit quiet for one moment, I'll have a look at you!

(*Crosses to L. end of cabinet as if to look for instrument.*

MADGE, *just as* DOCTOR *is at L., not before, advances near to the old* GENTLEMAN *up C. looking at him closely. She suddenly seems to be satisfied of something, backs away form C. to L. turning at L.C.,*

*and reaching out as if to get to the window L. and give
signal, then coming face to face with* WATSON *as he
turns and smiling pleasantly at him. Business with
glove. She begins to glide downstage, making a sweep
around toward door on R. side as if to get out. She
shows by her expression that she has recognized*
HOLMES, *but is instantly herself again, thinking possibly that* HOLMES *is watching her, and she wishes to
evade suspicion regarding her determination to get off
at door R. Quick as a flash the old* GENTLEMAN *springs
to the door down R., and stands facing her. She stops
suddenly on finding him facing her, then wheels
quickly about and goes rapidly across toward window
down L.*)

HOLMES

Oh, madam, a friend in need is a friend indeed, a friend indeed
—I wonder, pretty lady would you . . .

    (*Sharp*)

Don't let her get to that window.

    (WATSON, *who had moved up a little above windows
on L., instantly springs before the windows.* MADGE
stops on being headed off in that direction)

WATSON

Is that *you*, Holmes?

    (MADGE *stands motionless near L.C.*)

HOLMES

Quite so.

    (*Takes off his wig, etc.*)

WATSON

But, Holmes, what do you want me to do?

HOLMES

(*Easily*)

That's all, you've done it. Don't do anything more just now.

(MADGE *gives a sharp look at them, then goes very slowly for a few steps to C., and suddenly turns and makes a dash for door up C.*)

WATSON

Look out, Holmes! *She can get out through there.*

(*A step or two up.*

MADGE *runs off at door up C.* HOLMES *is unmoved*)

HOLMES

No, I don't think so.

(*Saunters over to above* WATSON's *desk. Suddenly seeing cigarettes on desk*)

Ah! I'm glad to see that you keep a few prescriptions carefully done up.

(*Picks up a cigarette and sits on desk*)

Good for the nerves!

(HOLMES *finds matches and lights cigarette.*

Enter the DRIVER *at door up C.*)

FORMAN

(*Speaking at once—so as to break in on* HOLMES)

I've got her, sir!

(*Very brief pause*)

WATSON

Good heavens! *Forman?* Is that you?

(HOLMES *nods "Yes"*)

WATSON

Well, really . . .

HOLMES

Has Inspector Bradstreet arrived with his men?

FORMAN

Yes, sir. One of 'em's in the hall there 'olding her. The others are in the kitchen garden. They came in over the back wall from Mortimer Street.

HOLMES

One moment.

(*Sits in thought*)

My dear Doctor—

(WATSON *moves toward* HOLMES *at desk*)

As you doubtless gather from the little episode that has just taken place, we are now making the arrests. The scoundrels are hot on my track. To get rid of me is the one chance left to them—and I take advantage of their mad pursuit to draw them where we can quietly lay our hand on them—one by one. We've made a pretty good haul already—four last night in the gas chamber—six this afternoon in various places, but I regret to say that up to this time the Professor himself has so far not risen to the bait.

WATSON

Where do you think he is now?

HOLMES

He's probably in the open streets, under some clever disguise watching for a chance to get at me.

WATSON

And was this woman sent in here?

HOLMES

Quite so. A spy—to let them know by some signal, probably at that window—

(*Pointing L.*)

WATSON

The blinds.

HOLMES

—if I was in the house. Forman!

> (*Motions him to come down.*
>
> *Voice lower. Business*)

Bring that Larrabee woman back here for a moment. When I take a fresh cigarette—let go your hold on her—carelessly—as if your attention was distracted. Pick her up again when I say.

FORMAN

Very good, sir!

> (*Exits quickly at door up C. Outside.*
>
> *Re-enters at door up C. bringing* MADGE LARRABEE *to down R.C.*)

Mrs. Larrabee, lads. Mr. Holmes would like a word with her. Thank you very much, lads.

> (*They stop.* MADGE *calm, but looks at* HOLMES *with the utmost hatred. Brief pause*)

HOLMES

Ah, Mrs. Larrabee—

> (MADGE, *who has looked away, turns to him angrily*)

—I took the liberty of asking you to come back in here for a moment—

> (*Puffs cigarette, which he has nearly finished*)

—in order to convey to you in a few fitting words—my sincere sympathy in your rather—unpleasant—predicament.

MADGE

> (*Hissing it out angrily between her teeth*)

It's a lie! A lie! There's no predicament.

HOLMES

Ah—I'm charmed to gather—from your rather forcible—observation—that you do not regard it as such. Quite right, too. Our
prisons are very well conducted nowadays. They're quite as comfortable as most of the hotels. They are certainly quieter and
more orderly.

MADGE

How the prisons are conducted is no concern of mine! There is
nothing they can hold me for—nothing!

HOLMES

(*Putting fresh cigarette in mouth*)

There may be something in that. Still—it occurred to me that you
might prefer to be near your unfortunate husband—eh?

(*Rises from table and goes up C. to gas burner. Slight,
good-natured chuckle*)

We hear a great deal nowadays about the heroic devotion of
wives, and all that—

(*Lights cigarette at gas*)

—rubbish. You know, Mrs. Larrabee, when we come right down
to it—you'd've done a great deal better on your own. If your
partner in life and crime had a fault . . . (*etc.*)

(FORMAN *carelessly relinquishes his hold on* MADGE's
*arm, and seems to have his attention called to door R.
Stands as if listening to something outside.* MADGE
gives a quick glance about and at HOLMES, *who is
lighting a cigarette at the gas, and apparently not no-
ticing anything. She makes a sudden dash for the window down L., quickly snaps up blind and makes a
rapid motion up and down before window with right
hand—then turns quickly, facing* HOLMES *with trium-
phant defiance.* HOLMES *is still lighting cigarette*)

HOLMES

(*To Forman*)

That's all, Forman. Pick her up again.

(FORMAN *at once goes to* MADGE *and turns her down L. and waits in front of window—holding her right wrist*)

Doctor, pull the blind down. I don't want you shot from the street.

(WATSON *instantly pulls down blind.*

NOTE: *Special care must be exercised regarding these window blinds. They must be made specially strong and solid, so that no failure to operate is possible*)

MADGE

(*Down L. in triumph*)

Ah! It's too late.

HOLMES

Too late, eh?

(*Strolling a little down C.*)

MADGE

The signal is given. You will hear from him soon.

HOLMES

(*Up C.*)

It wouldn't surprise me at all.

(*Door bell rings R.*

Voices of BILLY *and* PARSONS *outside R. Door R. at once opened, and* BILLY *on a little way, but held back by* PARSONS *for an instant. He breaks away from* PARSONS *and comes R.C. All very quick,* BILLY *dressed as a street gamin, and carrying a bunch of evening papers.* PARSONS *stands R.*)

HOLMES

(*As* BILLY *comes to R.C.*)

I expect to hear from him *now*.

(*Shout*)

Let—

(BILLY *stands panting*)

—him go, Parsons. Quick, Billy.

(BILLY *comes close to* HOLMES)

BILLY

He's just come, sir.

HOLMES

From where?

BILLY

The house across the street; he was in there a-watchin' these windows. He must 'ave seen something, for he's just come out—

(*Breathlessly R.C.*)

There was a cab waitin' for the doctor—and he's changed places with the driver.

HOLMES

Where did the driver go?

BILLY

He slunk away in the dark, sir, but he ain't gone far, an' there's two or three more 'angin' about.

HOLMES

(*Slight motion of the head toward* FORMAN)

Another driver!

BILLY

They're all in it, sir, an' they're a-layin' to get you in that cab w'en you come out, sir! But don't you do it, sir!

HOLMES

Get out again, Billy. Keep you eyes peeled.

BILLY

(*R.*)

Yes, sir—thank you, sir!

(*Exit at door R.*)

HOLMES

Watson, can you let me have a heavy portmanteau for a few moments—?

(MADGE *now watching for another chance to get at the window*)

WATSON

(*Up L.*)

Parsons—go and fetch my large Gladstone bag.

PARSONS

(*R.*)

Sir!

(*Exit at door R.*)

WATSON

I'm afraid it's a pretty shabby-looking . . .

(MADGE *suddenly tries to break loose from* FORMAN *and attempts to make a dash for window at L.* FORMAN *turns and pulls her a step or two away. Slight pause*)

MADGE

Let me go!

HOLMES

Many thanks, Mrs. Larrabee, but your *first* signal is all that we require. By it you informed your friend Moriarty that I was here in the house. You now wish to signal that there is danger. There *is* danger, Mrs. Larrabee, but I don't care to have you let him know it. Take her out, Forman; make her comfortable and happy.

> (FORMAN *leads* MADGE *up to door C. as if to take her out. She pulls him to a stop when up at C. and gives* HOLMES *a look of the most violent hatred.* HOLMES *is R.*)

HOLMES (*Continued*)

And tell the inspector to wait. I could send him one more. You can't tell!

FORMAN

Come along now!

> (*Takes her off at door up C.*
>
> As MADGE *is pulled up C., she snaps her fingers in* HOLMES's *face and goes off laughing hysterically*)

HOLMES

That's a fine woman! But . . . her crime is commonplace.

> (*Enter* PARSONS *at door R., carrying a large portmanteau or Gladstone valise*)

Put it down there.

> (*Pointing down before him at floor L. of C.*)

Thank you.

(PARSONS *put portmanteau down as indicated L.C.*)

Parsons, you ordered a cab for the doctor. It has been waiting, I believe.

PARSONS

Yes, sir, I think it 'as.

HOLMES

Be so good as to tell the driver, the one you'll now find there, to come in here and get a valise. When he comes tell him this is the one.

(*Exit* PARSONS *at door R.*)

WATSON

But surely he won't come in.

HOLMES

Surely he must! It's his one chance to get me into that cab! He'll take almost any risk for that.

(*Goes to above desk*)

HOLMES (*Continued*)

In times like this you should tell your man never to take the first cab that comes—

(*Smokes*)

—nor yet the second—the third—

WATSON

Yes, but in this case—

HOLMES

In this case I admit that I take advantage of the fact that I speak for your future guidance. Well, good-by, old fellow!

(*Shakes hands with him warmly and bringing him down L. a little*)

I'll write you from Paris but be so good as to keep me fully informed as to the future course of events.

(MORIARTY *enters at door R. in the disguise of a cabman, and goes at once to valise which* PARSONS *points out, trying to hurry it through and keeping face away from* HOLMES *but fidgeting about, not touching valise.* PARSONS *goes out*)

HOLMES

(*Speaks right on, apparently paying no attention to* MORIARTY)

As for these papers, I'll attend to them personally. Here, my man—

(*To* MORIARTY)

—help me to tighten these straps, will you—

(*He slides over to valise and kneels, pulling at strap, and* MORIARTY *bending over and doing same*)

There are a few little things in this bag—

(*Business*)

that I wouldn't care to have go missing—

HOLMES (*Continued*)

(*Looking around for an instant*)

And, you never can tell, the railways are so unreliable nowadays.

(MORIARTY *quickly looks up without lifting hands from valise, and at the same instant the snap of handcuffs is heard, and he springs up with the irons on his wrist, making two or three violent efforts to break loose. He then stands motionless R.C.* HOLMES *drops into chair C., a cigarette in his mouth.* MORIARTY *in rising knocks his hat off and stands facing audience.*

Music stops)

HOLMES

(*In a very quiet tone*)

Doctor, pray be so good as to strike upon the bell two or three times in rapid succession.

(WATSON *steps to desk and gives several rapid strokes of the bell.*

Enter FORMAN *at door up C.* FORMAN *goes down to* MORIARTY *and fastens handcuffs which he has on his own wrists to chain attached to that of* MORIARTY'S. *This is held an instant—the two men looking at each other*)

Forman!

FORMAN

Yes, sir.

HOLMES

Got a man there with you?

FORMAN

Yes, sir, the inspector came in himself, sir.

HOLMES

Ah—the inspector himself. We shall read graphic accounts in to-morrow morning's papers of the difficult and dangerous arrest he made at Dr. Watson's house in Kensington. Take him out, Forman, and introduce them—they'll be charmed to meet.

(FORMAN *starts to force* MORIARTY *off and up R.C.* MORIARTY *hangs back and endeavors to get at* HOLMES *—a very slight struggle*)

HOLMES (*Continued*)

No, wait! See what he wants!

MORIARTY

(*Low voice—R.C., moves C. to* HOLMES)

Do you imagine, Mr. Holmes, *that this is the end?*

HOLMES

I ventured to dream that it might be.

MORIARTY

Are you quite sure the police will be able to hold me?

HOLMES

I am quite sure of nothing.

MORIARTY

Ah!

(*Slight pause*)

I have heard you're planning to take a little trip—you and your friend here—a little trip on the Continent.

HOLMES

And if I do?

MORIARTY

(*A step to* HOLMES)

I shall meet you there.

(*Slight pause.* FORMAN *moves up to door C., quietly with* MORIARTY. *Stopping at door*)

You will change your course—you will try to elude me—but whichever way you turn—there will be eyes that see and wires that tell. I shall meet you there—and you know it. And when I fall, you will fall with me.

(*Exit* FORMAN *and* MORIARTY)

WATSON

We could give up the trip, Holmes . . .

HOLMES

Was ever such a dreary dismal and unprofitable world? Crime is commonplace, existence is commonplace and no qualities save the commonplace have any future on this earth. But I mustn't indulge my morbid fantasies now. The worst is yet to come.

WATSON

(Embarrassed; takes watch out)

The worst? Good heavens, Holmes, we've barely five minutes left to get to Baker Street; your appointment with Sir Edward and the Count . . . to rescue that package of letters.

HOLMES

No, it is all right. They are coming here.

WATSON

Here?

HOLMES

That is, if you will be so good as to permit it.

WATSON

Certainly—but why not at Baker Street?

HOLMES

The police wouldn't let us through the ropes.

WATSON

Police and ropes!

HOLMES

Police—ropes—ladders—hose—crowds—fire engines—

WATSON

Good heavens, Holmes, you don't mean to say . . .

HOLMES

(*Nods*)

Quite so—the villains have burnt me out.

WATSON

Oh, that's too bad. What did you lose?

HOLMES

Everything! Oh, I'm so glad of it! This one thing—that I must do—here in a few moments—is the end.

(HOLMES *rises*)

WATSON

Oh, you mean—Miss Faulkner?

(*Going to lower corner of desk.*

HOLMES *nods slightly in affirmative without turning to* WATSON.

Love music. Very soft)

HOLMES

(*Turning suddenly to* WATSON)

Watson—there were four to one against me! They said "*Come here.*" I said "*Stay close to me,*" and she did! She clung to me—you know, I could feel her heart beating against mine. As I knew she would . . . she trusted me—and I was playing the game! You see it is a dangerous game—but I must play it! It'll be the same tonight! She'll be there—I'll be here! She'll listen—she'll believe—she'll trust me—and I'll—be playing—the game. *No—* I've had enough! This is my last case.

(WATSON *has been watching him narrowly*)

Oh well! what does it matter? Life's a brief affair at best—a few sunrises and sunsets—the warm breath of a few summers—the cold chill of a few winters—

(*Looking down on floor a little way before him in meditation*)

And then—

    (*Pause*)

WATSON

And then—?

    (HOLMES *glances up at him. Upward toss of hand before speaking and goes R.*)

HOLMES

And then.

    (*The music stops*)

WATSON

    (*Going to* HOLMES *R.C.*)

My dear Holmes—I'm afraid that little trick of—gaining her confidence and regard went a little futher than you intended—

    (HOLMES *nods assent slightly*)

HOLMES

    (*Mutters after nodding*)

A trifle!

WATSON

For her—or for you?

HOLMES

Oh, for her—

    (*Looks up at* WATSON *slowly*)

and—for me.

WATSON

    (*Astonished. After an instant's pause*)

But—if you both love each other—

HOLMES

Love! Who spoke that word? Love is an emotional thing and is therefore opposed to the true, cold reason which I place above all things. I should never marry myself, lest I bias my judgment. Women are never to be trusted entirely, not the best of them. I can assure you that the most winning woman I ever knew was hanged for poisoning her three little children for the insurance money. No, no, I must cure Miss Faulkner of her regard for me while there's still time. She's coming here.

WATSON

She won't come alone?

HOLMES

No, Térèse will be with her.

> (HOLMES *turns and goes up C., and to door up L., getting a book on the way, and placing it in the way of door closing. Turns to* WATSON *up L.*)

When she comes let her wait in that room. I'm sure you can manage that.

> (*Bell.* HOLMES *and* WATSON *look at one another. Going up C. to door*)

She may be there now. Can I go to your dressing room, and brush away some of this dust?

WATSON

By all means!

> (*Goes to door up C. on the L. side of* HOLMES)

My wife is in the drawing room. Do look in on her a moment— it will please her so much.

HOLMES

> (*At door*)

It will more than please me!

(Opens door. Piano heard off when the door is opened)

Home! Love! Life! Ah, Watson!

(Eyes glance about, thinking. Exits.

WATSON *turns and goes to his desk—not to sit. Enter* PARSONS *at door R.)*

PARSONS

Excuse me, sir, a young lady wants to speak to you most urgent. If there's anyone 'ere she won't come in.

WATSON

Did she give any name?

PARSONS

No, sir. I asked her and she said it was unnecessary—as you wouldn't know 'er. She 'as 'er maid with 'er, sir.

WATSON

Then it must be—show her in.

(PARSONS turns to go)

And, Parsons—

(PARSONS stops and turns)

WATSON *(Continued)*

(Lower voice)

Two gentlemen, Count von Stalburg and Sir Edward Leighton will call. As soon as they arrive send them in here and send at once for Mr. Holmes . . . He's in my dressing room.

PARSONS

Yes, sir.

WATSON

Send everybody else away—I'll see that lady now.

PARSONS

Yes, sir.

(Exit at door R. Brief pause. PARSONS *appears outside door R., showing some one to the room.*

Enter at door R., ALICE FAULKNER.

ALICE *glances apprehensively about, fearing she will see* HOLMES. *Seeing that* WATSON *is alone, she is much relieved and goes toward him.* PARSONS *closes R. door from outside)*

ALICE

(With some timidity)

Is this—Dr. Watson's room?

WATSON

(Encouragingly—and advancing a step or two)

Yes, and I am Dr. Watson.

ALICE

Is—could you tell me if Mr. Holmes—Mr. Sherlock Holmes—is here?

WATSON

He will be before long, Miss—er—

ALICE

My name is Faulkner.

WATSON

Miss Faulkner. He arrived a short while ago, but has gone upstairs for a few moments.

ALICE

Oh!—

(With an apprehensive look)

—and is he coming down—soon?

WATSON

Well, the fact is, Miss Faulkner, he has an appointment with two gentlemen, and I was to let him know as soon as they arrived.

ALICE

Do you suppose I could wait—without troubling you too much —and see him—*afterward?*

WATSON

Certainly.

ALICE

Thank you—and I—I don't want him to know—that I came.

WATSON

Of course, if you wish, there's no need of my telling him.

ALICE

It's—very important *indeed* that you *don't* tell him, Dr. Watson. I can explain it all to you afterward.

WATSON

No explanation is necessary, Miss Faulkner.

ALICE

Thank you.
(*Glances about*)
I suppose there is a waiting room for patients?

WATSON

Yes, or you could sit over there in my dispensary.
(*Indicating door up L.*)
You'll be less likely to be disturbed.

ALICE

Thank you, yes.
(ALICE *glances toward door up L.*)

I think I would rather be—where it's entirely quiet.

(*Bell of front door outside R. rings*)

WATSON

(*Going to door up L., above desk*)

Then step this way. I think the gentlemen have arrived.

(*Stands up L. at door*)

ALICE

(*Goes to door up L., and turns*)

And when the business between the gentlemen is over, could you please have someone tell me?

WATSON

I'll tell you myself, Miss Faulkner.

ALICE

Thank you.

(*She exits at door up L.*

WATSON *moves a little to R.* PARSONS *enters at door R.*)

PARSONS

Count von Stalburg, and Sir Edward Leighton.

(*Enter* SIR EDWARD *and* COUNT VON STALBURG *at door R. Exit* PARSONS *at door R., closing it after him*)

WATSON

Count—Sir Edward—

(*Bowing and coming forward near C.*)

SIR EDWARD

Dr. Watson.

(*Bows*)

Good evening.

(*Placing his hat on pedestal R.*

VON STALBURG *bows slightly and stands R.*)

Our appointment with Mr. Holmes was changed to your house, I believe.

WATSON

Quite right, Sir Edward. Pray be seated, gentlemen.

(SIR EDWARD *sits in the chair R.C.* WATSON *sits near L.C., R. of desk*)

VON STALBURG

Mr. Holmes is a trifle late.

(*Sits R., below* SIR EDWARD)

WATSON

He has already arrived, Count. I have sent for him.

VON STALBURG

Ugh!

(*Slight pause*)

SIR EDWARD

It was quite a surprise to receive his message an hour ago changing the place of meeting. We should otherwise have gone to his house in Baker Street.

WATSON

You would have found it in ashes, Sir Edward.

SIR EDWARD

What! Really!

VON STALBURG

(*Surprise*)

Ugh!

(*Both looking at* WATSON)

SIR EDWARD

The house burnt!

WATSON

Burning, now probably.

SIR EDWARD

I'm terribly sorry to hear this. It must be a severe blow to him.

WATSON

No, he minds it very little.

SIR EDWARD

(*Surprised*)

Really! I should hardly have thought it.

VON STALBURG

Do I understand you to say, Doctor, that you have sent for Mr. Holmes?

WATSON

Yes, Count, and he'll be coming shortly. Indeed, I think I hear his step upon the stair now.

(*Pause. Enter* HOLMES *at door up C. He is very pale. His clothing is rearranged and cleansed, though he still, of course, wears the clerical suit, white tie, etc. He stands up C. near door a moment.* SIR EDWARD *and* COUNT *rise and turn to him.* WATSON *rises and goes to desk, where he soon seats himself in chair behind desk.* SIR EDWARD *and the* COUNT *stand looking at* HOLMES. *Brief pause*)

HOLMES

Gentlemen, be seated again, I beg. Our business tonight can be very quickly disposed of. You were notified to meet me here this evening in order that I might—

(*Pause*)

HOLMES (*Continued*)

—place in your hands the package which you engaged me—on behalf of your exalted client—to recover. I must say, in justice to myself, that but for that agreement on my part, and the consequent steps which you took upon the basis of it, I could never have continued with the work. As it was, however, I was bound to do so, and therefore pursued the matter—to the very end—and I now have the honor to deliver it.

SIR EDWARD

(*Formally*)

Permit me to congratulate you, Mr. Holmes, upon the marvelous skill you have displayed, and the promptness with which you have fulfilled your agreement.

VON STALBURG

Oh! No! No! No!

SIR EDWARD

(*Stopping examination and looking across to* HOLMES)

What does this mean?

(*Pause.* HOLMES *turns to* SIR EDWARD *in apparent surprise*)

VON STALBURG

These letters!!

SIR EDWARD

And these—other things. Where did you get them?

HOLMES

I purchased them—last night.

SIR EDWARD

Purchased them?

HOLMES

Quite so.

VON STALBURG

From whom—if I may ask?

HOLMES

From whom? From the parties concerned—by consent of Miss Faulkner.

VON STALBURG

You have been deceived.

HOLMES

What!

(WATSON *rises and stands at his desk*)

VON STALBURG

(*Excitedly*)

This packet contains nothing—not a single letter or paper that we wanted. All clever imitations! The photographs are of another person! You have been duped. In spite of your supposed cleverness, they have tricked you.

SIR EDWARD

Most decidedly duped, Mr. Holmes! Oh, dear Lord, what will the minister say.

(HOLMES *turns quickly to* SIR EDWARD, *R.C.*)

HOLMES

Oh, this is terrible!

(*Turns back to L. and to* WATSON. *Stands looking in his face*)

SIR EDWARD

(*Astonished*)

Terrible! Surely, sir, you do not mean by that, that there is a possibility that you may not be able to recover them!

(*Enter* ALICE *at door up L., and stands listening*)

HOLMES

I'm afraid that that is quite true!

SIR EDWARD

After your positive assurance! After the steps we have taken in the matter by your advice!

(*Turns to* COUNT, *too indignant to speak*)

VON STALBURG

(*Indignantly*)

Surely, sir, you don't mean there is no hope of it?

HOLMES

I'm afraid that there is none whatever, Count, Miss Faulkner has clearly changed her mind . . .

SIR EDWARD

Why, this is scandalous! It is criminal, sir! Have you any idea what this will mean in terms of diplomatic consequences for Her Majesty's government. You had no right to mislead us in this way, and you shall certainly suffer the consequences. I shall see to it that you are brought into court to answer for it, Mr. Holmes. It will be such a blow to your reputation that you—

HOLMES

There is nothing more to say, Sir Edward—I am ruined— ruined—

ALICE

(*Coming forward L.C.*)

He is not ruined, Sir Edward.

HOLMES

Gentlemen—

(*Putting watch back in pocket*)

My letter promised the packet for a quarter-past nine. It is fourteen and one-half minutes past.

SIR EDWARD/VON STALBURG

(*Starting up with admiration and delight as they perceive the trick*)

Ah! Excellent! Admirable, Mr. Holmes! It is all clear now! Really marvelous!

(*To one another, etc.*)

Yes—upon my word.

(*On* SIR EDWARD *and* COUNT *breaking into expressions of admiration,* WATSON *quickly moves up to them R.C., and stops them with a quick "Sh!" All stand motionless.* HOLMES *and* ALICE *looking at one another.* HOLMES *goes quickly to* ALICE *and puts the package into her hands*)

HOLMES

(*As he does this*)

Take it! It is yours. Never give it up. Use it only for what you wish!

(*Stop music*)

SIR EDWARD

(*Springing forward with a mild exclamation*)

What! We are not to have it.

(*Throwing other package up stage to R.

VON STALBURG *gives an exclamation or look with fore-going*)

HOLMES

(*Turning from* ALICE *but keeping left hand back upon her hands into which he put the package—as if to make her keep it. Strong—breathless—not loud—with emphatic shake of the head*)

You are not to have it.

SIR EDWARD

After all this?

HOLMES

After all this.

VON STALBURG

But, my dear sir—

SIR EDWARD

This is outrageous! Your agreement?

HOLMES

I break it!—warrants—summons—arrests—will find me here. Watson, get them out! Get them away!

(*Stands at R. of* WATSON'S *desk, his back to audience. Brief pause.* WATSON *moves toward* SIR EDWARD *and the* COUNT *at the back of* HOLMES)

WATSON

I'm sure, gentlemen, that you will appreciate the considerable strain under which Mr. Holmes has been working.

ALICE

(*Stepping toward C.—interrupting*)

Wait a moment, Dr. Watson!

(*Going to* SIR EDWARD)

Here is the package, Sir Edward!

(*Hands it to* SIR EDWARD *at once, R.C.*

WATSON *motions to* PARSONS *off R. to come on*)

HOLMES

(*Turning to* ALICE)

No!

(*Down a little*)

ALICE

(*To* HOLMES)

Yes—

(*Turning to* HOLMES. *Pause*)

I much prefer that he should have them. Since you came to me that night and asked me to give them to you, I've thought of what you said. You were right—it was revenge.

(*She looks down a moment—then suddenly turns away to L. and stands down L.*)

SIR EDWARD

We are greatly indebted to you, Miss Faulkner—

(*Looks at* VON STALBURG)

VON STALBURG

To be sure! To be sure!

SIR EDWARD

And to you, too, Mr. Holmes—if this was a part of the game. It was certainly an extraordinary method of obtaining possession of valuable papers—but we won't quarrel with the method as long as it accomplished the desired result! Eh, Count?

(*Placing package in breast pocket and buttoning coat*)

VON STALBURG

Certainly not, Sir Edward.

(WATSON moves up near R.C.)

SIR EDWARD

(Turning to HOLMES*)*

You have only to notify me of the charge for your services—

(ALICE gives a little look of bitterness at the word "Charge")

—Mr. Holmes, and you will receive a check. I have the honor to wish you—good night. Miss Faulkner . . . Dr. Watson . . . This way, Count . . .

(WATSON bows and follows them to door R. HOLMES does not move. COUNT VON STALBURG bows to HOLMES and to WATSON and exits at door R., followed by SIR EDWARD. PARSONS exits after giving SIR EDWARD his hat. WATSON quietly turns and sees HOLMES beckoning to him. WATSON goes to HOLMES up C., who whispers to him, after which he quietly exits at C. door. HOLMES, after a moment's pause, looks at ALICE and then goes down L.C.)

HOLMES

(Speaks hurriedly)

Now that you think it over, Miss Faulkner, you are doubtless becoming aware of a series of tricks by which I sought to deprive you of your property. I could not take it out of the house that night—of course, you could have recovered it at law. I therefore resorted to a cruel and cowardly device to induce you to relinquish it.

ALICE

(Not looking at him)

But you—you did not give it to them—

(Pause)

HOLMES

(*In a forced, cynical, hard voice*)

No, of course not . . . it was necessary that you should do, as you did.

ALICE

What?

(ALICE *looks suddenly up at him in surprise and pain, with a breathless "What?" scarcely audible.*
HOLMES *meets her look without a tremor*)

HOLMES

(*Slowly, distinctly*)

You see, it was a trick—a deception—to the very end.

(ALICE *looks in his face a moment longer and then down*)

Your maid is waiting.

(*Indicating R. with slight motion, at the same time going toward R.C.*)

ALICE

(*Stopping him as he is going R. by speech—no action*)

And was it—a trick—last night—when they tried to kill you?

HOLMES

(*Hearing* ALICE, *stops dead*)

I went there to purchase the counterfeit package—to use as you have seen.

ALICE

And—did you know that I would come?

(*Pause*)

HOLMES

No.

(Coming down L.C. a trifle below ALICE*)*

*(*ALICE *gives a subdued breath of relief)*

HOLMES *(Continued)*

But it fell in with my plans notwithstanding. Now that you see me in my true light, Miss Faulkner, there is nothing left to say but good night—and good-by—which you ought to be very glad to do. Please believe, I meant no harm to you—it was purely business. For that you see I would sacrifice everything. Even my supposed—friendship for you—was a—pretense . . . a sham.

(She has slowly turned away to the front, a little L.,
during his speech. She turns and looks him in the face)

ALICE

(Quietly but distinctly)

I don't believe you.

(They look at one another)

HOLMES

(After a while)

Why not?

ALICE

From the way you speak—from the way you—look—from all sorts of things!—

(With a very slight smile)

You're not the only one—who can tell things—from small details.

HOLMES

(Coming a step closer to her)

Your powers—of observation—are somewhat remarkable, Miss Faulkner—and your deduction is quite correct! I suppose—indeed I know—that I love you. I love you. But I know as well what I am—and what you are—

(ALICE *begins to draw nearer to him gradually, but with her face turned front*)

I know that no such person as I, seared drugged, poisoned, almost at an end should ever dream of being a part of your sweet life! Just beginning it would be a crime for me to think it. There is every reason why we should say good-by and farewell! There is every reason—

(ALICE *gently places her right hand on* HOLMES's *breast, which stops him from continuing speech. He suddenly stops. After an instant he begins slowly to look down into her face. His left arm gradually steals about her. He presses her head close to him and the lights fade away with* ALICE *resting in* HOLMES's *arms, her head on his breast*)

CURTAIN